The Perfect Blend!

The Perfect Blend!

smoothies and juices
to delight and inspire

LOVE FOOD

This is a Love Food book
Love Food is an imprint of Parragon Books Ltd
First published in 2007

Parragon Publishing
Queen Street House
4 Queen Street
Bath BA1 1HE
United Kingdom

ISBN: 978-1-4054-8648-4

Printed in China

Designed by Talking Design
Photography by Günter Beer
Home Economist Stevan Paul
Additional recipes and text by Linda Doeser

NOTES FOR THE READER

This book uses metric and imperial measurements. Follow the same units of measurement throughout; do
not mix metric and imperial.

All spoon measurements are level: teaspoons are assumed to be 5 ml, and tablespoons are assumed
to be 15 ml.

Unless otherwise stated, milk is assumed to be full fat, eggs and individual vegetables such as potatoes
are medium, and pepper is freshly ground black pepper.

Recipes using raw or very lightly cooked eggs should be avoided by infants, the elderly, pregnant women,
convalescents and anyone suffering from an illness.

Contents

Introduction

DRINKING FLAVORED MILK AND FRUIT JUICES IS CERTAINLY NOTHING NEW, BUT TODAY'S GENERATION OF SMOOTHIES AND JUICES REFLECT A LEVEL OF SOPHISTICATION TYPICAL OF THE TWENTY-FIRST CENTURY LIFESTYLE. CONTEMPORARY TASTES TOGETHER WITH A CONCERN FOR HEALTHIER OPTIONS IN THE DIET HAVE RESULTED IN INNOVATIVE COMBINATIONS OF FLAVORS PLUS THE USE OF FRESH INGREDIENTS.

Smoothies trace their ancestry back to the milkshakes of the last century and they are probably descendants of the eighteenth-century milk punch. To begin with milk was flavored with a variety of spirits, brandy being particularly popular, then the milkshake—milk whisked with ice cream—was invented. This was further enhanced with the addition of extra flavorings, such as fruit. With the phenomenal development of artificial flavorings and colorings, the milkshake degenerated into a chemical mix that had never been near a strawberry or banana and was often sickly sweet. It finally came of age with the smoothie, usually based on milk or other dairy products and flavored with fresh fruit or vegetables, or a combination of both. Herbs and spices often add extra zing to the mix, appealing to adult palates as well as to children and young people.

Fruit and, to a lesser extent, vegetable juices have always been valued thirst quenchers. Understandably, easily squeezed fruits, such as oranges, were the most common and, generally, the juice was served on its own. Sometimes, other flavorings were incorporated, perhaps the most familiar being a dash of Worcestershire sauce in tomato juice. Gradually, the ease and convenience of commercially produced juices made fresh juice virtually obsolete in most homes. However, one positive thing that happened at the same time was that in their search for a greater share of the market, manufacturers started to produce mixed juices, such as a combination of tropical fruits. Now, with our desire for more subtle flavors and our nutritional awareness, fresh fruit and vegetable juices, often in the form of exotic "cocktails" have returned to the domestic kitchen.

Just because we know what is good for us doesn't mean that we always do what is right. For example, we all know that nutritionists recommend five portions of fruit and vegetables a day and most people recognize that it is important to start the day with breakfast. However, life is lived in the fast lane these days and it is difficult to fit in shopping and cooking with the demands of work and family life. Smoothies and juices can make a considerable contribution to resolving this dilemma. They can be made in minutes, so saving precious time in the kitchen. They are full of nutrients and count towards the "five a day". Many are positive powerhouses and provide a real energy boost first thing in the morning or at any time when you feel that you are running out of steam.

Happily, smoothies and juices are the exception to the popular "rule" that it won't do you any good if it doesn't taste nasty. On the contrary, the flavors burst deliciously in the mouth, whether sweet or savory. Teenagers regard them as "cool" so they are an argument-free, easy alternative to sugar-packed fizzy sodas. Kids—even those who loathe vegetables and have to be cajoled into eating a piece of fruit—love them, especially modern milkshakes which have been reinvented in the wake of the smoothie. For those who don't want alcoholic drinks, they offer an exciting and adult alternative at social gatherings. They can play a useful role in a calorie-controlled diet and may help anyone trying to give up smoking without gaining weight by substituting a candy-eating habit.

The recipes in this book include a wide range of both sweet and savory treats and are divided into five chapters. Energy Explosion! is the one to turn to in the morning when you need to kick-start the day or when you're pushed for time and simply can't fit making a snack into your schedule. Health Booster! is packed with recipes for maximizing your wellbeing, offering easy and tasty ways to revitalize your looks and refresh a sluggish system. These smoothies and juices are great for keeping you in tip-top condition and are both tempting and nutritious for anyone recovering from an illness. The astonishing range of thirst-quenching and refreshing juices in Juicy Joy! is indeed a colorful and luscious delight that will spoil you for choice. When your energy is flagging and the day begins to drag, turn to Perfect Pick-Me-Ups! for a timely reviver. Finally, Super Shakes! is for children of all ages with both family favorites and great new ideas.

Fruit

FRUIT FORMS THE BASIS OF THE MAJORITY OF SMOOTHIES AND JUICES,

ALTHOUGH VEGETABLES ALSO PLAY AN IMPORTANT ROLE.

Apple: a good source of dietary fiber, apples contain some vitamin A and C. Eating apples have a natural sweetness and juiciness, especially Braeburn, Empire, McIntosh, and Red Delicious. Choose apples that smell fragrant and avoid any damaged specimens. Apples combine well with berries, carrots, and other orchard fruits.

Banana: packed with energy and extremely nutritious, bananas are a rich source of niacin, riboflavin, and potassium, and contain vitamins A and C. They combine well with berries, nuts, pit fruits, and other tropical fruits. The small Lady Finger or Sugar bananas are especially sweet. Always use ripe bananas for smoothies and shakes.

Blueberry: a rich source of vitamin C and also containing iron, blueberries are deliciously sweet and juicy. Choose plump berries with a characteristic bloom. Frozen blueberries can also be used in smoothies.

Grapefruit: one grapefruit will provide more than the adult daily requirement of vitamin C. The juice is particularly refreshing but often quite sour. The variety Sweetie does not require extra sweetening and both pink and ruby grapefruit tend to be sweeter than white ones. Choose firm, ripe fruits as they will be juicy.

Guava: exceptionally high in vitamin C, guavas are also a good source of niacin and potassium. There are several varieties, all with a sweet-sour flavor and aromatic flesh. They combine well with apples and other tropical fruit.

Kiwi fruit: these are very rich in vitamin C and also contain vitamin E. The seeds are edible. Choose plump fruit which will be juicy. The enzymes in kiwi fruit will cause dairy products to curdle. They combine well with berries and other tropical fruit.

Mango: a good source of vitamins A and C, mangoes also contain beta-carotene. There are thousands of varieties—Bombay is particularly juicy. Choose fragrant fruit that yields when gently pressed. Mangoes go well with melon, coconut, and other tropical fruits.

Melon: as they have a high water content, melons are great for smoothies and juices. Orange-fleshed varieties contain carotene, an anti-oxidant that can help protect against some diseases. Most varieties are suitable for making drinks—Cantaloupe and Charentais, both orange-fleshed varieties, are especially fragrant and flavorful. Buy fruit that feels heavy and smells sweet. Melon combines well with berries, pineapple, cucumber, mint, ginger, and other varieties of melon.

Orange: all citrus fruits, including tangerines and their hybrids, are very rich in vitamin C. Only sweet oranges are suitable for drinks (bitter varieties are used for marmalade and savory sauces). An ideal variety is Valencia, which is very juicy and has few pits, and blood oranges provide extra color. Avoid damaged or shriveled oranges as they will be dry. Oranges combine well with berries, pit fruits, and other citrus fruit.

Passion fruit: a source of vitamins A and C, passion fruit has a sweet-sour flavor. The seeds are edible but the pulp may be strained. Choose firm, slightly wrinkled fruit that feels heavy and do not store in the refrigerator. Passion fruit combines well with berries and other tropical fruits.

Peach: a source of vitamins A, B, and C, peaches have a natural sweetness. They may be white or yellow—choose whichever you prefer. Always buy ripe peaches (they do not ripen after picking) and do not store for more than 2 days. Peel and pit them before use. They combine well with nuts and most other fruit, especially raspberries.

Pear: an orchard fruit containing some riboflavin, potassium, and vitamins A and C, pears come in a wide variety of shapes and sizes. Especially juicy varieties include Bartlett, Packham's, and Red Bartlett. Buy ripe fruit but avoid any that is squashy. Pears go well with most other fruit.

Pineapple: rich in vitamin C, pineapples also contain an enzyme that breaks down protein so the juice is an aid to digestion. It is a sweet fruit with a slightly acerbic edge to it. There are many varieties, not usually sold by name. Choose a plump fruit and test for ripeness by gently pulling out one of the bottom leaves. Do not store it in the refrigerator. It combines well with melon, other tropical fruit, coconut, and tropical spices, such as ginger and cinnamon.

Raspberry: a good source of vitamin C, niacin, riboflavin and potassium, raspberries have long been credited with healing properties. There are many varieties, all of which are fragrant and juicy. Buy evenly colored fruit and do not store for longer than 2 days. Raspberries combine particularly well with peaches and also with melon and other berries.

Strawberry: probably the world's most popular soft fruit, strawberries contain iron, potassium, and vitamins B and C. There are many different varieties and all are sweet and succulent, especially if locally grown. Choose ripe fruit that has not been squashed. Don't wash strawberries as they will become waterlogged and do not store for more than 24 hours. Strawberries combine well with peaches, bananas, pineapples, and other berries.

Watermelon: containing some vitamin B and C, watermelons have a very high water content and a refreshing flavor. Sugar Baby is a particularly sweet variety. Choose firm fruit that does not sound hollow when tapped. Watermelon combines well with lemon, orange, grapefruit, and other melons.

Essential Equipment

MOST OF THE EQUIPMENT REQUIRED FOR MAKING SMOOTHIES, JUICES, AND SHAKES WILL ALREADY EXIST IN ANY REASONABLY WELL-EQUIPPED KITCHEN. NO SPECIALIST EXPENSIVE TOOLS ARE REQUIRED, ALTHOUGH YOU MIGHT LIKE TO CHOOSE SOME THAT SPEED THINGS UP OR MAKE LIFE A LITTLE EASIER. REMEMBER THAT YOU WILL NEED TO HAVE ADEQUATE STORAGE SPACE FOR ANY EXTRA EQUIPMENT WHEN IT IS NOT IN USE.

Blender

This is the most expensive piece of equipment you will require for making smoothies, juices, and milkshakes and is a worthwhile investment in any kitchen. A detachable goblet fits on to a base that houses the motor. Small blades in the goblet whirl around chopping finely or reducing ingredients to a purée. There is usually a feeder tube or removable cover that allows you to add ingredients, usually a liquid, while the motor is running. Most blenders have at least 2 speeds and all modern domestic models have safety features. Food processors or liquidizers can be also be used.

Juicers

Although the recipes featured in this book do not require an electric juicer the investment in one could be very worthwhile. These machines offer you a fast and efficient way to produce good quantities of juice with the minimum of effort. Simply chop the fruit or vegetables into small enough pieces to fit in the juicer, turn it on and watch as the juicer automatically separates the juice from the pulp and skin leaving you with a clean and tasty glass of juice. On some models you don't even have to peel or core the fruit!

Chopping boards

Always keep a separate board for preparing fruit and vegetables and never use it for poultry, meat, or fish. Wooden boards look attractive and do the least damage to knife blades. They cannot be sterilized but this is not an important consideration for one kept exclusively for fruit and vegetables. Polyethylene boards, which come in a range of colors, can be sterilized and are dishwasher-proof. They have rough surfaces to prevent both food and board from slipping.

Citrus press

A classic dome-shaped lemon squeezer is easiest to use and inexpensive. A cone-shaped press is very efficient.

Corer

Short and long corers are available. You simply push the circular cutting edge through the center of the fruit or vegetable and withdraw the core in the cylinder. As fruit and vegetables are usually sliced or chopped for drinks, you can remove the cores of such fruit as apples with a paring knife at the same time.

Grater

A standard box grater is suitable for all kinds of grating and slicing, including grating citrus rind, the most likely use when preparing drinks. A special citrus grater, made from acid-resistant stainless steel, is also available.

Knives

A range of cook's knives is essential for any type of food preparation, including making drinks. It is better to buy them separately than as a set, testing the balance of each by holding it in your hand. Heavy, but well-balanced knives are more efficient and easier to use than light ones. A cook's knife, with a wide, curved blade 20–25 cm/8–10 inches long, is an all-purpose tool and can be used for hefty tasks, such as slicing fruit and vegetables, as well as light ones, such as chopping herbs. A utility knife is a slightly smaller version with a 13–18-cm/5–7-inch-long blade and is useful for light slicing and chopping. A paring knife, with a similar shaped blade 8–10 cm/3^{1}/$_{4}$–4 inches long, is ideal for peeling and scraping fruit and vegetables, and for slicing and chopping small items. It is very useful for preparing ingredients, such as oranges, peaches, and root ginger, for smoothies.

Store knives in a knife block rather than a drawer where they will be a danger to fingers and liable to damage. A steel or knife sharpener helps keep them in good condition.

Sieves and strainers

A range of different sizes is useful in any kitchen. Use a nylon sieve for acidic fruits as metal may taint the flavor.

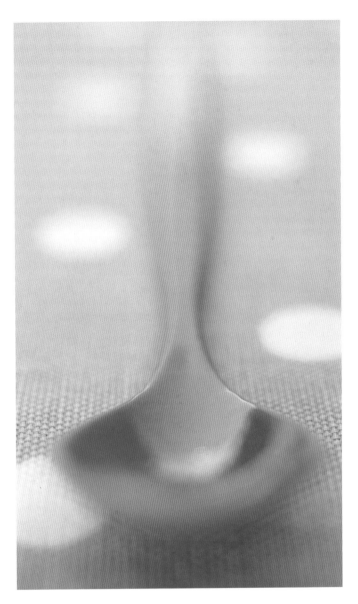

Vegetable peelers

There are three basic types – swivel, V-shaped, and Y-shaped – all of which make it easier than using a knife to peel fruit and vegetables thinly. Which type you choose is a matter of taste, but left-handed people should check that the sharp edge works for them or buy a special left-handed version.

Top 10 Tips for Smoothie Success

1 Use the freshest possible, ripe ingredients. Overripe or damaged fruit will not improve by being made into a smoothie.

2 Use fruit and vegetables that are in season and, preferably, locally grown for the best flavor and greatest natural sweetness.

3 Don't prepare fruit and vegetables in advance, as they will start to dry out and lose their juiciness. Some vitamins are quickly destroyed on exposure to air so this would also reduce the nutritional value—one of the great benefits of smoothies.

4 Smoothies are best served chilled, but adding ice will dilute them. Keep milk and other dairy products in the refrigerator until required. Chill the glasses before you make the smoothie. If you want to add ice to the blender, crack it first to avoid damaging the blades. Put ice cubes in a plastic bag, wrap it in a clean dish towel, and hit with a hard object or swing against a hard wall that won't be damaged.

5 When adding strongly flavored spices, such as ground ginger or chiles, err on the side of caution. Add half the suggested quantity, taste, and add more if you like.

6 Never overfill the blender goblet; check the manufacturer's instructions for the maximum capacity for your particular model. Overfilling may result in liquid spilling out of the top and/or the ingredients being inadequately combined. About half full is best for smoothies, so if necessary, make them in batches.

7 To save time and for even mixing, chop ingredients into pieces about the same size. They don't have to be finely diced but should be fairly small.

8 When measuring spoonfuls of honey, the most popular sweetener for smoothies, dip the spoon in hot water first. This makes it easier to get all the honey into the mixture rather than leaving half of it behind. This is also a good idea with ice-cream scoops if you are using ice cream straight from the freezer for shakes.

9 Use fresh herbs whenever possible, but if the one you require is not available, substitute a similar one or use frozen herbs. Dried herbs do not work in smoothies.

10 Don't be afraid to experiment. Try substituting different berries, a flavored yogurt for plain, or, if you are cutting down on your intake of fat, skim milk for whole milk.

Top 10 Benefits of Smoothies & Juices

1 Using fresh fruit and vegetables in prime condition ensures optimum nutritional value.

2 Smoothies are an easy and delicious way to increase your intake of fruit and vegetables—a direct way toward a healthier diet for all the family.

3 There are no artificial flavors, colors, or preservatives, some of which are known to have adverse effects on people with allergies and on children.

4 Fruit and some vegetables, particularly carrots and beet, are naturally sweet so smoothies are an easy way to reduce sugar intake without compromising taste.

5 They take hardly any time to make, yet provide an instant energy boost and quench your thirst.

6 They offer a tasty and interesting alternative to commercial products, cost less, are usually healthier, and can be adapted to your personal taste.

7 You can drink them any time of day from breakfast to bedtime and they provide a far better, longer-lasting, and healthier snack when your energy is flagging than potato chips, chocolate, or cookies.

8 They're a great way of using up odd pieces of fruit—the last banana in the bowl or a few grapes left on the stem—providing they are still in good condition.

9 You know exactly what ingredients have been used, so there are no unpleasant surprises or hidden quantities of saturated fats or sugar.

10 They taste fabulous!

Energy Explosion!

Banana Breakfast Shake

GET YOUR DAY OFF TO A HEALTHY START WITH THIS QUICK BUT NUTRITIOUS BANANA SHAKE. BANANAS ARE A GREAT SOURCE OF POTASSIUM, WHICH IS SAID TO PLAY A ROLE IN CONTROLLING HIGH BLOOD PRESSURE.

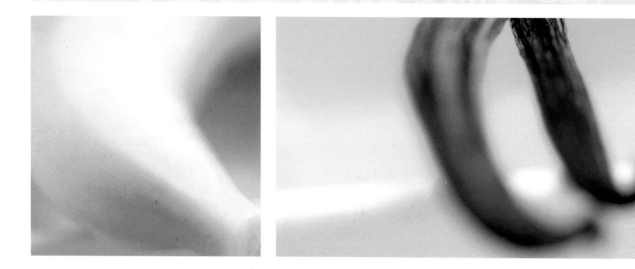

SERVES 2

2 RIPE BANANAS
3/4 CUP YOGURT
1/2 CUP SKIM MILK
1/2 TSP VANILLA EXTRACT

Put the bananas, yogurt, skim milk, and vanilla extract into a food processor or blender and process until smooth.

Serve at once.

Breakfast Bar

FRUITY DRINKS PROVIDE A GREAT PICK-ME-UP AT ANY TIME OF DAY AND ARE PERFECT FOR GIVING AN ENERGY BOOST FIRST THING IN THE MORNING.

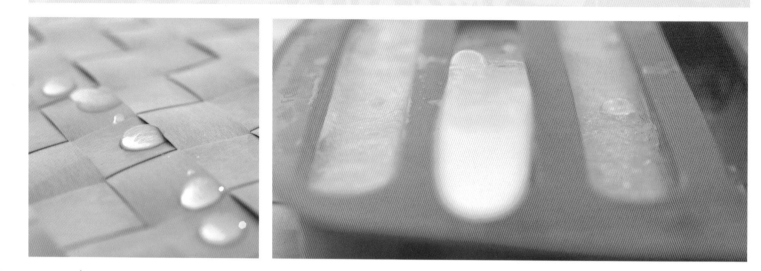

SERVES 4

14 OZ/400 G CANNED GRAPEFRUIT
   AND ORANGE SEGMENTS
4 TBSP LEMON JUICE
3 TBSP LIME JUICE
SCANT 2 CUPS ORANGE
   JUICE, CHILLED

Tip the canned fruit and the can juices into a food processor or blender. Add the lemon, lime, and orange juice and process until smooth.

Pour into chilled glasses and serve.

Rise & Shine Juice

VEGETABLES MAY NOT BE THE FIRST THING YOU THINK OF FOR A BREAKFAST DRINK,
BUT THIS JUICE IS PACKED WITH NUTRIENTS AND IS A GREAT WAY TO START YOUR
"FIVE-A-DAY."

SERVES 1

4 TOMATOES, QUARTERED
SCANT $^1/_2$ CUP GRATED CARROT
1 TBSP LIME JUICE

Put the tomatoes, carrot, and lime juice into a food processor or blender and process for a few seconds until smooth.

Place a nylon strainer over a bowl and pour in the tomato mixture. Using a spoon, gently push as much of the liquid through the strainer as possible. Discard any pips and pulp remaining in the strainer.

Pour the juice into a glass and serve at once.

Breakfast Smoothie

KICK-START YOUR DAY WITH THIS RICH VITAMIN- AND MINERAL-PACKED
ENERGIZER.

SERVES 2

1 CUP ORANGE JUICE

1/2 CUP PLAIN YOGURT

2 EGGS

2 BANANAS, SLICED AND FROZEN

DECORATION

WHOLE BANANAS, OR SLICES
   OF BANANA

Pour the orange juice and yogurt into a food processor or blender and process
gently until combined.

Add the eggs and frozen bananas and process until smooth.

Pour the mixture into glasses and decorate the rims with whole bananas or
slices of banana. Serve.

Wake Up Sweetie

Sweetie grapefruit and ugli fruit are very similar — a hybrid of grapefruit, they are sweeter and juicier, perfect to wake you up in the morning.

SERVES 2

3 LARGE RIPE SWEETIE GRAPEFRUIT
  OR UGLI FRUIT
2/3 CUP SPARKLING WATER
1 TBSP FLOWERY HONEY (OPTIONAL)

DECORATION
SOME SLICES OF LIME OR
  PEELED KIWI FRUIT
2 TBSP PLAIN YOGURT

Halve and squeeze the fruit into two glasses.

Add water and honey (if you like).

Serve with a slice or two of lime or kiwi, floated on the surface and topped with a spoon of yogurt.

Berry Brightener

THIS ENERGIZING SMOOTHIE IS A GREAT WAY TO KICK-START THE DAY. ADD 1–2 TSP OF HONEY IF YOU PREFER YOUR SMOOTHIES A LITTLE SWEETER.

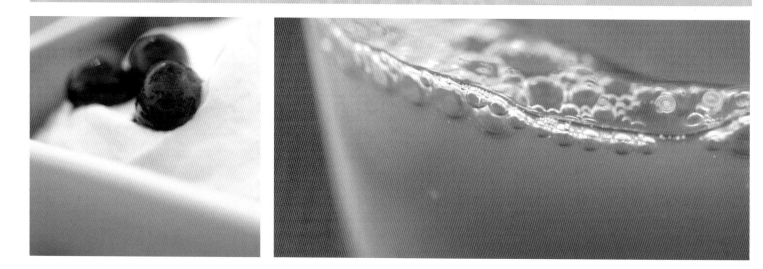

SERVES 2

1^1/$_2$ CUPS BLUEBERRIES
^{2}/$_3$ CUP CRANBERRY JUICE
^{2}/$_3$ CUP PLAIN YOGURT

Put the blueberries and cranberry juice into a food processor or blender and process for 1–2 minutes, until smooth.

Add the yogurt and process briefly to combine. Taste and add honey, if you like. Process briefly again until thoroughly blended.

Pour into chilled glasses, add straws and serve.

Tropical Watermelon Smoothie

THE PERFECT CHOICE FOR A SUMMERY DAY — IT WILL BOOST YOUR VITALITY AND QUENCH YOUR THIRST FROM SUNRISE TO SUNSET.

SERVES 2

1 WATERMELON WEDGE, ABOUT
  1 LB 5 OZ
2 SMALL BANANAS, PREFERABLY
  LADY FINGER
1 CUP COCONUT CREAM

Remove and discard the seeds from the watermelon, then cut the flesh off the rind, and chop coarsely. Peel and slice the bananas.

Put the watermelon, bananas, and coconut cream in a food processor or blender and process until combined.

Pour into chilled glasses and serve.

Raspberry & Strawberry Smoothie

POSSIBLY TWO OF THE MOST POPULAR FRUITS COME TOGETHER IN THIS DELICIOUS

MIX — A TASTE SENSATION.

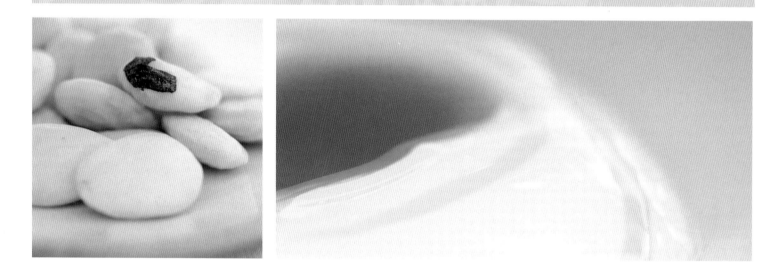

SERVES 2–4

1/3 CUP RASPBERRIES

1/2 CUP STRAWBERRIES, HALVED

1 CUP PLAIN YOGURT

1 CUP MILK

1 TSP ALMOND EXTRACT (OPTIONAL)

2–3 TBSP HONEY, TO TASTE

Press the raspberries through a nylon strainer into a bowl using the back of a spoon. Discard the seeds in the strainer.

Put the raspberry purée, strawberries, yogurt, milk, and almond extract if using into a food processor or blender, and process until smooth and combined.

Pour the smoothie into chilled glasses, stir in honey to taste, and serve.

Ruby Anyday

TOO GOOD JUST FOR TUESDAYS, THIS IS RUBY ANYDAY.

SERVES 2

1 LARGE RIPE PINK OR RUBY GRAPEFRUIT
SCANT 1/2 CUP ICE-COLD WATER
SCANT 1/2 CUP STRAINED PLAIN YOGURT
1 TBSP FLOWERY HONEY, SUCH
   AS ACACIA

DECORATION
SLICES OF PINK OR RUBY GRAPEFRUIT

Cut the grapefruit into fourths, then pull off the peel and as much pith as possible. Discard any seeds.

Put the grapefruit and water into a food processor or blender and process until smooth. Add the yogurt and honey and process again until combined.

Pour into glasses, decorate with slices of grapefruit, and serve at once.

Blueberry Thrill

BLUEBERRIES ARE STILL A MUCH UNDERRATED PLEASURE. IN THIS SMOOTHIE THEIR RAW, TART SWEETNESS IS ENHANCED BY THE YOGURT.

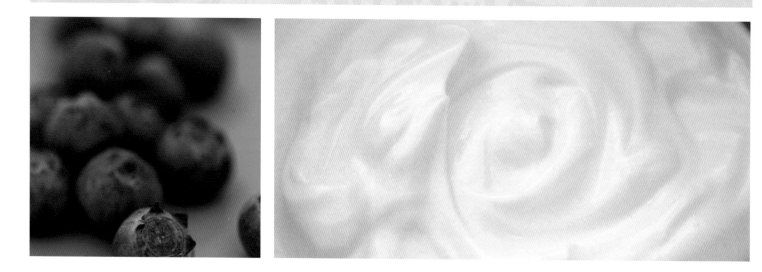

SERVES 2

SCANT $^1/_2$ CUP STRAINED PLAIN YOGURT

SCANT $^1/_2$ CUP WATER

SCANT 1 CUP FROZEN BLUEBERRIES

DECORATION

WHOLE FROZEN BLUEBERRIES

Put the yogurt, water, and blueberries into a food processor or blender and process until smooth.

Pour into glasses and top with whole frozen blueberries.

Orange & Strawberry Cream

THE IMPECCABLE COMBINATION OF FRESH FLAVORS MAKES THIS ONE OF THE

MOST POPULAR SMOOTHIES.

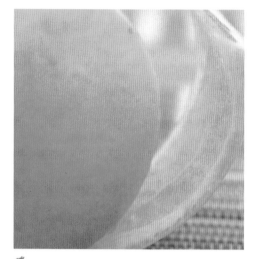

SERVES **2**

$^1/_2$ CUP PLAIN YOGURT

$^3/_4$ CUP STRAWBERRY YOGURT

$^3/_4$ CUP ORANGE JUICE

SCANT 1$^1/_4$ CUPS FROZEN
   STRAWBERRIES

1 BANANA, SLICED AND FROZEN

DECORATION

SLICES OF ORANGE AND WHOLE FRESH

   STRAWBERRIES ON COCKTAIL STICKS

Pour the plain and strawberry yogurts into a food processor or blender and process gently. Add the orange juice and process until combined.

Add the strawberries and banana and process until smooth.

Pour the mixture into tall glasses and decorate with slices of orange and whole strawberries on cocktail sticks.

Fruit Kefir

SUBSTITUTE THE PEACH YOGURT FOR A FLAVOR OF YOUR CHOICE TO TRY A

DIFFERENT OPTION OF THIS DELICIOUS BLEND.

SERVES 4

1 BANANA
1 CUP STRAWBERRIES, HALVED
1 CUP PEACH YOGURT
2 TBSP HONEY
1 CUP APPLE JUICE, CHILLED

Peel the banana and slice it directly into a food processor or blender.

Add the strawberries, yogurt, and honey and process until smooth. With the motor running, pour in the apple juice through the hole in the lid.

Pour into chilled glasses and serve.

Berry Smoothie

THE BERRIES GIVE THIS SMOOTHIE A RICH SHADE OF PINK, MAKING IT A GREAT TREAT TO SERVE AT KIDS' PARTIES.

SERVES 2

1¹/₄ CUPS WHOLE MILK
   OR SOY MILK
2 TBSP PLAIN YOGURT
1 TBSP MAPLE SYRUP
3 BLACKBERRIES
³/₈ CUP BLUEBERRIES
¹/₄ CUP BLACK CURRANTS

DECORATION
ROASTED SESAME SEEDS

Place all the ingredients in a blender or food processor and process until combined and frothy.

Pour into tall glasses, sprinkle the roasted sesame seeds over the top and serve immediately.

Almond & Banana Smoothie

THIS IS A GREAT SMOOTHIE FOR THOSE FOLLOWING A DAIRY-FREE DIET, BUT THERE IS CERTAINLY NO COMPROMISE ON TASTE.

SERVES 3–4

SCANT 1 CUP WHOLE BLANCHED
   ALMONDS
2 1/2 CUPS DAIRY-FREE MILK
2 RIPE BANANAS, HALVED
1 TSP NATURAL VANILLA EXTRACT
GROUND CINNAMON, FOR SPRINKLING

Put the almonds into a food processor or blender and process until very finely chopped. Add the milk, bananas, and vanilla extract and blend until smooth and creamy.

Pour into glasses and sprinkle with cinnamon.

Banana, Peach & Strawberry Smoothie

THIS SMOOTHIE REQUIRES A LITTLE PREPARATION AS YOU WILL NEED TO PEEL THE

PEACH, BUT THE RESULT IS WELL WORTH IT.

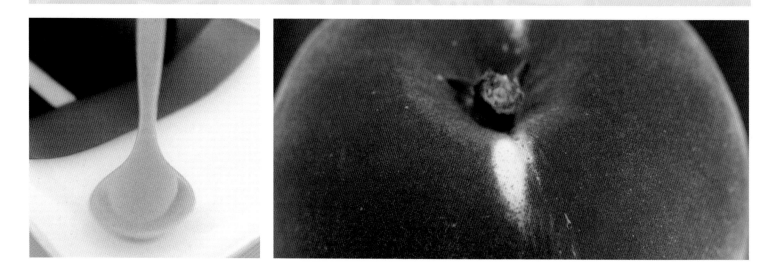

SERVES 2

1¹/₄ CUPS WHOLE MILK
   OR SOY MILK

2 TBSP PLAIN YOGURT

1 TBSP MAPLE SYRUP

¹/₂ PEELED AND SLICED BANANA

¹/₂ STONED, PEELED, AND
   CHOPPED PEACH

3 HULLED STRAWBERRIES

Place all the ingredients in a blender or food processor and process until combined and frothy.

Pour into glasses and serve immediately.

Orchard Fruit Smoothie

THE VERY BRIEF COOKING OF THE FRUIT JUST MELLOWS THE FLAVORS, AND LETS

THE COLORS FROM THE DAMSONS AND PLUMS SEEP INTO THE APPLES AND PEARS.

SERVES 2

1 RIPE PEAR, PEELED AND CUT
   INTO FOURTHS
1 APPLE, PEELED AND CUT INTO
   FOURTHS
2 LARGE RED PLUMS, HALVED
   AND PITTED
4 RIPE DARK PLUMS, HALVED
   AND PITTED
GENEROUS 3/4 CUP WATER

DECORATION
SLICES OF APPLE OR PEAR

Put the pear, apple, plums, and water into a small pan. Cover tightly, then set over medium heat and bring slowly to a boil. Take off the heat and let cool. Chill.

Put the fruit and water into a food processor or blender and process until smooth.

Pour into glasses, decorate with slices of apple or pear and serve.

Melon & Pineapple Crush

WHEN YOU ARE FEELING JADED, THIS GLORIOUS PAIRING OF SWEET AND TART

FLAVORS WILL PERK YOU UP AND GIVE YOU A BOOST.

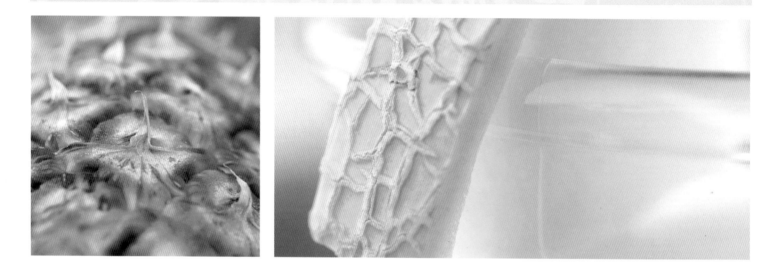

SERVES 2

SCANT $^1/_2$ CUP PINEAPPLE JUICE

4 TBSP ORANGE JUICE

$4^1/_2$ OZ/125 G GALIA MELON,

  CUT INTO CHUNKS

1 CUP FROZEN PINEAPPLE CHUNKS

4 ICE CUBES, CRUSHED

DECORATION

SLICES OF GALIA MELON

Pour the pineapple juice and orange juice into a food processor or blender and process gently until combined.

Add the melon, pineapple chunks, and ice cubes and process until a slushy consistency has been reached.

Pour the mixture into glasses and decorate with slices of melon.

Serve at once.

Carrot & Red Bell Pepper Booster

THIS DYNAMIC COMBINATION OF FLAVORS WILL FIRE UP YOUR SYSTEM AND BOOST YOUR ENERGY LEVELS.

SERVES 2

1 CUP CARROT JUICE

1 CUP TOMATO JUICE

2 LARGE RED BELL PEPPERS, DESEEDED AND COARSELY CHOPPED

1 TBSP LEMON JUICE

FRESHLY GROUND BLACK PEPPER

Pour the carrot juice and tomato juice into a food processor or blender and process gently until combined.

Add the red bell peppers and lemon juice. Season with plenty of freshly ground black pepper and process until smooth.

Pour the mixture into glasses, then add straws and serve.

Tomato Blazer

TANGY AND A LITTLE BIT HOT, THIS IS A JUICE WITH A BIT OF GET-UP-AND-GO!

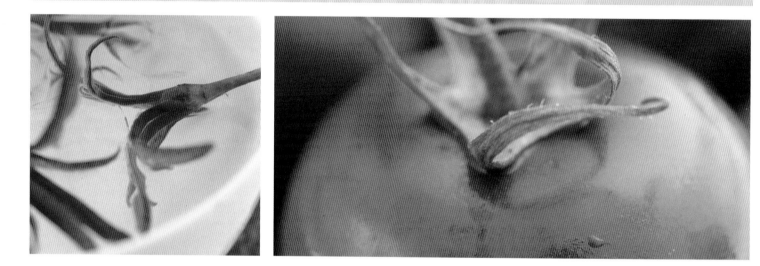

SERVES 2

GENEROUS 2 CUPS TOMATO JUICE

DASH OF WORCESTERSHIRE SAUCE

1 SMALL RED CHILE, DESEEDED
  AND CHOPPED

1 SCALLION, TRIMMED AND CHOPPED

6 ICE CUBES, CRUSHED

DECORATION

2 LONG, THIN RED CHILES,
  CUT INTO FLOWERS

To make the chile flowers, use a sharp knife to make six cuts along each chile. Place the point of the knife about 1/2 inch/1 cm from the stem end and cut toward the tip. Put the chiles in a bowl of iced water and let stand for 25–30 minutes, or until they have spread out into flower shapes.

Put the tomato juice and Worcestershire sauce into a food processor or blender and process gently until combined. Add the chopped chile, scallion, and ice cubes and process until smooth.

Pour the mixture into glasses and garnish with the chile flowers.

Vegetable Cocktail

THIS SAVORY COCKTAIL COMBINES ALL THE GOODNESS OF FRESH VEGETABLES IN ONE GLASS.

SERVES 2

1/2 CUP CARROT JUICE

1 LB 2 OZ/500 G TOMATOES, SKINNED, DESEEDED, AND COARSELY CHOPPED

1 TBSP LEMON JUICE

4 CELERY STALKS, TRIMMED AND SLICED

4 SCALLIONS, TRIMMED AND COARSELY CHOPPED

SCANT 1/3 CUP FRESH PARSLEY

SCANT 1/3 CUP FRESH MINT

DECORATION

2 LEAFY CELERY STICKS

Put the carrot juice, tomatoes, and lemon juice into a food processor or blender and process gently until combined.

Add the sliced celery along with the scallions, parsley, and mint and process until smooth.

Pour the mixture into glasses and garnish with leafy celery sticks.

Serve at once.

Health Booster!

Sweet & Sour Smoothie

BOOST YOUR IMMUNE SYSTEM AND HELP COUNTERACT THE EFFECTS OF THE

PASSING YEARS WITH THIS DELICIOUS AND COLORFUL SMOOTHIE.

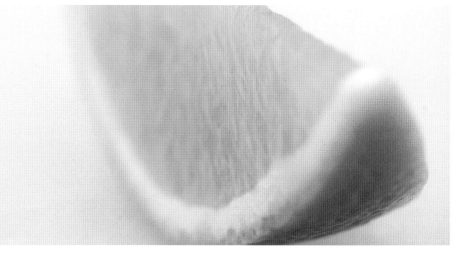

SERVES 2

1 CUP FRESHLY SQUEEZED
  ORANGE JUICE
1 CUP COOKED BEET, CHOPPED
5 TBSP PLAIN YOGURT
2/3 CUP WATER
SALT (OPTIONAL)

DECORATION
CHOPPED BEET

Put the orange juice, beet, and yogurt into a food processor or blender and add the water. Process until smooth and thoroughly combined.

Pour the smoothie into a chilled pitcher and stir in salt to taste (if using).

Decorate with chopped beet and serve.

Papaya & Banana Smoothie

THIS PACKS A REAL NUTRITIONAL PUNCH, YET IS ESPECIALLY EASY TO DIGEST, SO IT'S THE PERFECT DRINK FOR ANYONE RECOVERING FROM ILLNESS OR FATIGUE.

SERVES 2

1 PAPAYA
JUICE OF 1 LIME
1 LARGE BANANA
1 1/2 CUPS FRESHLY SQUEEZED
   ORANGE JUICE
1/4 TSP GROUND GINGER

Halve the papaya and scoop out and discard the gray-black seeds. Scoop out the flesh and chop coarsely, then toss with the lime juice. Peel and slice the banana.

Put the papaya, banana, orange juice, and ginger into a food processor or blender and process until thoroughly combined. Pour into chilled glasses and serve.

Detox Special

WHEN YOUR HAIR IS LANK, YOUR SKIN LOOKS DULL AND YOU JUST DON'T FEEL YOURSELF, A RESTORATIVE — AND DELICIOUS — INTAKE OF VITAMINS A AND C IS JUST WHAT THE DOCTOR ORDERED.

SERVES 2

1 MANGO
4 KIWI FRUIT
1 1/2 CUPS PINEAPPLE JUICE
4 FRESH MINT LEAVES

Cut the mango into 2 thick slices as close to the pit as possible. Scoop out the flesh and chop coarsely. Cut off any flesh adhering to the pit. Peel the kiwi fruit with a sharp knife and chop the flesh.

Put the mango, kiwi fruit, pineapple juice, and mint leaves into a food processor or blender and process until thoroughly combined. Pour into chilled glasses and serve.

Apple & Celery Revitalizer

GIVE YOUR SPIRITS A LIFT AND YOUR HEART A BOOST WITH THIS TASTY VITALITY DRINK. IT IS ALSO REPUTED TO BE SOMETHING OF A HANGOVER CURE.

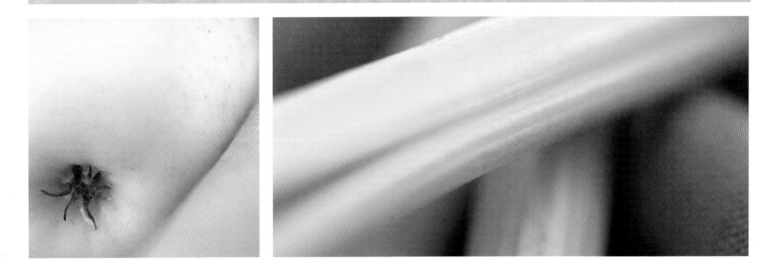

SERVES 2

1 EATING APPLE, PEELED, CORED, AND DICED

1 CUP CHOPPED CELERY

1¹/4 CUPS MILK

PINCH OF SUGAR (OPTIONAL)

SALT (OPTIONAL)

DECORATION

STRIPS OF CELERY

Put the apple, celery, and milk into a food processor or blender and process until thoroughly combined.

Stir in a pinch of sugar and some salt if you like.

Pour into chilled glasses, decorate with strips of celery, and serve.

Banana & Strawberry Smoothie

SIMPLE BUT DELICIOUS, THE STRAWBERRY MAKES YET ANOTHER APPEARANCE IN THIS
CLASSIC COMBINATION.

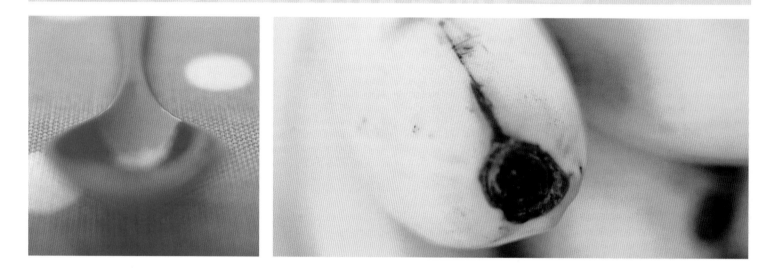

SERVES 2

1 BANANA, SLICED
1/2 CUP FRESH STRAWBERRIES,
   HULLED
GENEROUS 2/3 CUP PLAIN YOGURT

Put the banana, strawberries, and yogurt into a food processor or blender and process for a few seconds until smooth.

Pour into glasses and serve at once.

Tropical Smoothie

PINEAPPLE AND PAPAYA ARE RICH IN ANTI-OXIDANTS AND CONTAIN DIGESTIVE-SYSTEM STIMULATING ENZYMES.

SERVES 2

1 RIPE PAPAYA, PEELED, PITTED, AND
   CHOPPED
1/2 FRESH PINEAPPLE, PEELED AND
   CHOPPED
2/3 CUP SOY MILK
11/4 CUPS SOY YOGURT

DECORATION
CHOPPED PINEAPPLE

Place all the ingredients into a food processor or blender and process until smooth.

Pour into glasses, decorate with chopped pineapple and serve.

Apple, Carrot & Cucumber Juice

This drink is packed with anti-oxidants and soluble fiber, and the diuretic properties of cucumber and carrot help relieve fluid retention.

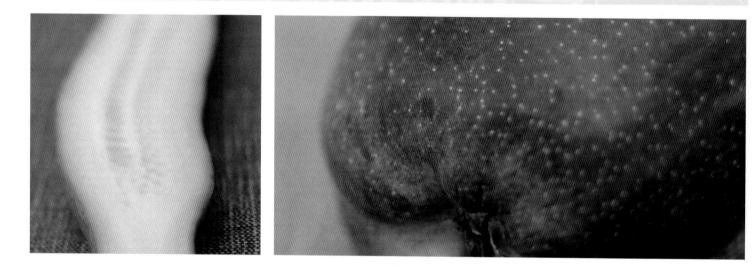

SERVES 1

1 APPLE, UNPEELED, CORED, AND
  CHOPPED
1 CARROT, PEELED AND CHOPPED
1/2 CUCUMBER, CHOPPED

DECORATION
PIECES OF CARROT, CUCUMBER,
  AND APPLE ON A COCKTAIL STICK

Place the ingredients into a food processor or blender and process.

Pour into a glass. Put the pieces of carrot, cucumber, and apple on to a cocktail stick and set on top of the glass. Serve.

Blueberry Dazzler

SWEET, SHARP, FRAGRANT, RICH, AND CREAMY — THIS IS PURE MAGIC IN A GLASS.

SERVES **2**

3/4 CUP APPLE JUICE

1/2 CUP PLAIN YOGURT

1 BANANA, SLICED AND FROZEN

GENEROUS 1 CUP FROZEN BLUEBERRIES

DECORATION

WHOLE FRESH BLUEBERRIES ON
  COCKTAIL STICKS

Pour the apple juice into a food processor or blender. Add the yogurt and process until smooth.

Add the banana and half of the blueberries and process well, then add the remaining blueberries and process until smooth.

Pour the mixture into tall glasses.

Decorate with whole fresh blueberries on a cocktail stick and serve.

Apricot & Orange Smoothie

THIS SMOOTHIE MAKES A GREAT VITAMIN- AND MINERAL-PACKED BREAKFAST IN A GLASS.

SERVES 2

1 CUP BOILING WATER
SCANT 1 CUP DRIED APRICOTS
JUICE OF 4 MEDIUM ORANGES
2 TBSP PLAIN YOGURT
1 TSP SOFT DARK BROWN SUGAR

Put the apricots in a bowl and pour the boiling water over them. Let them soak overnight.

In the morning, put the apricots and their soaking water into a food processor or blender and process until puréed. Add the orange juice to the apricots in the food processor, and process until combined.

Pour into glasses and top with 1 tablespoon of yogurt and a sprinkling of brown sugar.

Berry Booster

SESAME SEEDS ARE AN UNUSUAL ADDITION BUT THEY GIVE THIS SMOOTHIE A LITTLE SOMETHING EXTRA. SPRINKLE SOME OVER THE TOP TO DECORATE IF DESIRED.

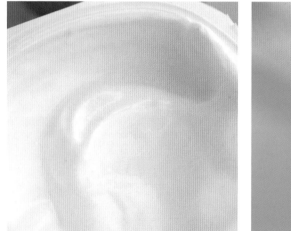 

SERVES 1

1/8 CUP BLUEBERRIES

3/8 CUP RASPBERRIES, THAWED
   IF FROZEN

1 TSP HONEY

SCANT 1 CUP PLAIN YOGURT

ABOUT 1 HEAPING TBSP CRUSHED
   ICE

1 TBSP SESAME SEEDS

Put the blueberries into a food processor or blender and process for 1 minute.

Add the raspberries, honey, and yogurt and process for an additional minute. Add the ice and sesame seeds and process again for an additional minute.

Pour into a tall glass and serve at once.

Guava Goodness

GUAVAS ARE REMARKABLY HIGH IN VITAMIN C AND WHEN BLENDED WITH MILK

PROVIDE A VERY NUTRITIOUS START TO ANY DAY.

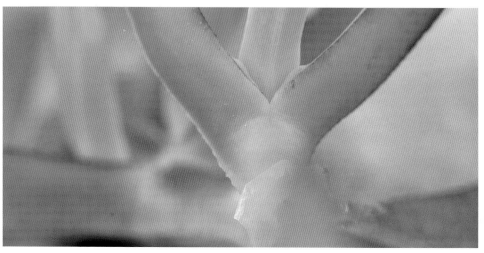

SERVES 2

14 OZ/400 G CANNED GUAVAS,
  DRAINED
1 CUP ICE-COLD MILK

Place the guavas into a food processor or blender and pour in the milk. Process until well blended.

Strain into glasses to remove the hard seeds. Serve.

Black & Blue

CULTIVATED BLACKBERRIES ARE CONSISTENTLY PLUMP AND JUICY, UNLIKE THEIR HEDGEROW COUSINS, WHICH CAN BE SUBSTITUTED IF YOU HAVE A GOOD SUPPLY.

SERVES 2

GENEROUS 3/4 CUP CULTIVATED
   BLACKBERRIES
SCANT 1 CUP BLUEBERRIES
SCANT 1/2 CUP ICE-COLD WATER
2/3 CUP PLAIN YOGURT

Put the blackberries, blueberries, water, and yogurt into a food processor or blender and process until smooth.

Pour into glasses and serve.

Pear & Raspberry Delight

PINK, LIGHT, AND FRUITY, THIS REFRESHING SMOOTHIE IS SIMPLY DELICIOUS. IF ... E THE SEEDS, YOU CAN USE A STRAINER TO MAKE IT SILKEN SMOOTH.

SERVES 2

2 LARGE RIPE ANJOU PEARS

SCANT 1 CUP FROZEN RASPBERRIES

GENEROUS 3/4 CUP ICE-COLD WATER

HONEY, TO TASTE

DECORATION

RASPBERRIES ON COCKTAIL STICKS

Peel the pears and cut into fourths, removing the cores. Put into a food processor or blender with the raspberries and water and process until smooth.

Taste and sweeten with honey if the raspberries are a little sharp.

Pour into glasses and decorate with whole raspberries on cocktail sticks and serve.

Mint & Cucumber Refresher

THIS IS GREAT TO SERVE AT A SUMMER PARTY—THE CUCUMBER INSIDE THE GLASS

WILL BE A REAL TALKING POINT!

SERVES 1

FEW SPRIGS OF MINT

1 TSP POWDERED SUGAR

JUICE 1 LIME

1-INCH PIECE CUCUMBER, THINLY
    SLICED

YOUR FAVORITE SPARKLING WATER,
    CHILLED

ICE CUBES

Chop a few sprigs of mint leaves and mix with the sugar.

Rub a little lime juice round the rim of a pretty glass and dip in the minted sugar. Leave to dry.

Mix the rest of the lime juice, cucumber, and mint — some chopped and some whole — in a pitcher and chill.

To serve, pour the lime and cucumber into the prepared glass and top up with chilled water to taste. Add ice cubes and serve.

Carrot Cocktail

PINEAPPLE AND CARROT ARE A DELICIOUS COMBINATION, PRODUCING A THICK AND
REFRESHING DRINK PACKED WITH VITAMINS.

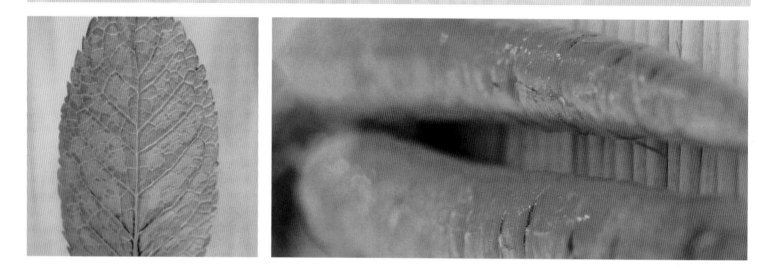

SERVES **1**

1/2 CUP RAW CARROTS, PEELED AND
  ROUGHLY CHOPPED

1 SLICE PINEAPPLE, ROUGHLY
  CHOPPED

1 TSP LEMON JUICE

1 TBSP HONEY

ICE

DECORATION

SPRIG OF PARSLEY OR MINT

Place the carrots, pineapple, lemon juice, and honey into a food processor or blender and process for 1-2 minutes until smooth.

Serve over ice with a sprig of parsley or mint.

24 Carrot

PINEAPPLE CONTAINS ENZYMES THAT NOT ONLY AID DIGESTION, BUT CAN EFFECTIVELY REDUCE INFLAMMATION AND SWELLING.

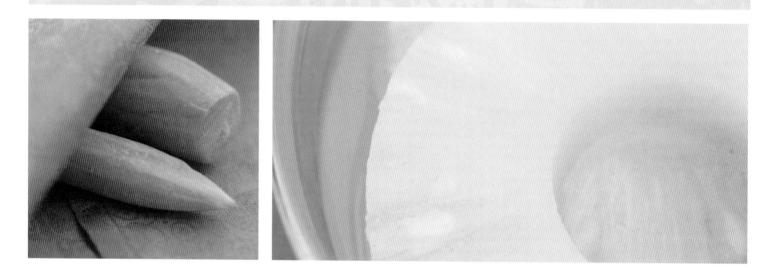

SERVES 2

HANDFUL OF CRACKED ICE
2 CARROTS, COARSELY CHOPPED
4 OZ/100 G CANNED PINEAPPLE
   PIECES IN JUICE, DRAINED
3/4 CUP PINEAPPLE JUICE, CHILLED

DECORATION
STRIPS OF CUCUMBER

Put the ice into a food processor or blender, add the carrots, pineapple pieces, and pineapple juice, and process until slushy.

Pour into chilled glasses and decorate with strips of cucumber.

On The Beat

BEET CONTAINS NO FAT, VERY FEW CALORIES, AND IS A GREAT SOURCE OF FIBER.

OMIT THE SALT IF YOU ARE BEING EXTRA HEALTHY.

SERVES 2

1 CUP COOKED BEET, CHOPPED
1/2 CUP ORANGE JUICE, CHILLED
5 TBSP PLAIN YOGURT, CHILLED
2/3 CUP STILL MINERAL WATER,
  CHILLED
SALT

DECORATION
SLICES OF ORANGE

Put the beet, orange juice, yogurt, and water into a food processor or blender and season to taste with salt.

Process until smooth, then pour into chilled glasses, and serve, decorated with slices of orange.

Beet, Pear & Spinach Juice

BEET STIMULATES THE LIVER AND HELPS TO CLEANSE THE DIGESTIVE SYSTEM. THE PEAR ADDS SWEETNESS AND FIBER. SPINACH CONTAINS ANTI-OXIDANTS THAT HELP TO ELIMINATE FREE RADICALS.

SERVES **1**

1 BEET, TRIMMED, PEELED, AND CHOPPED

1 PEAR, CORED AND CHOPPED

1/2 CUP (TIGHTLY PACKED) FRESH SPINACH LEAVES

DECORATION

SPINACH LEAF

Place the ingredients in a food processor or blender and process. Dilute with filtered water to taste.

Pour into a glass and decorate with the spinach leaf. Serve.

Carrot & Ginger Energizer

THIS STIMULATING BLEND OF FLAVORS IS GUARANTEED TO GIVE YOU A BOOST WHEN YOU NEED IT.

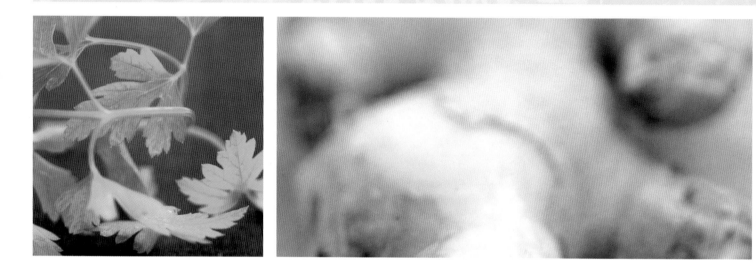

SERVES 2

1 CUP CARROT JUICE

4 TOMATOES, SKINNED, DESEEDED, AND COARSELY CHOPPED

1 TBSP LEMON JUICE

SCANT 1/3 CUP FRESH PARSLEY

1 TBSP GRATED FRESH GINGERROOT

6 ICE CUBES, CRUSHED

1/2 CUP WATER

DECORATION

CHOPPED FRESH FLAT-LEAF PARSLEY

Put the carrot juice, tomatoes, and lemon juice into a food processor or blender and process gently until combined.

Add the parsley to the food processor along with the ginger and ice. Process until well combined, then pour in the water and process until smooth.

Pour the mixture into tall glasses and garnish with chopped fresh parsley.

Serve at once.

Red Pepper Reactor

NOT FOR THE FAINT-HEARTED, THIS FIERY MIX WILL CERTAINLY WAKE YOU UP IF YOU'RE HAVING A MID-MORNING SNOOZE.

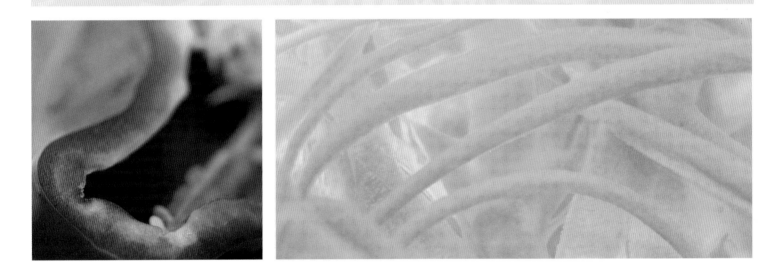

SERVES 2

1 CUP CARROT JUICE

1 CUP TOMATO JUICE

2 LARGE RED BELL PEPPERS, SEEDED AND COARSELY CHOPPED

1 TBSP LEMON JUICE

TO SERVE

FRESHLY GROUND BLACK PEPPER

DECORATION

STRIPS OF SHREDDED CARROT

Pour the carrot juice and tomato juice into a food processor or blender and process gently until combined.

Add the red bell peppers and lemon juice. Season with plenty of freshly ground black pepper and process until smooth.

Pour the mixture into glasses, decorate with strips of shredded carrot, and serve.

Juicy Joy!

Watermelon Refresher

A GREAT FAVORITE IN GREECE, WHERE ROADSIDE STALLS SELL ENORMOUS
WATERMELONS, THIS SMOOTHIE MAKES THE MOST OF THIS GIGANTIC FRUIT'S JUICINESS.

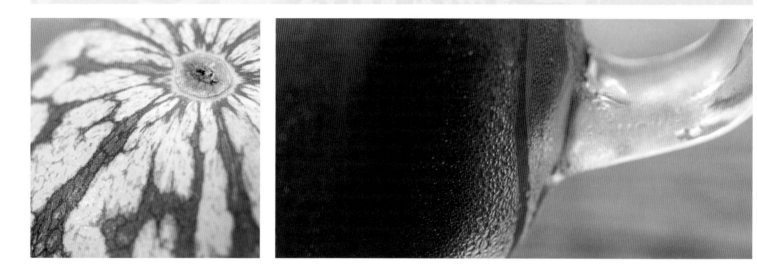

SERVES 2

1 WEDGE OF WATERMELON,
   WEIGHING ABOUT 12 OZ/350 G
ICE CUBES

DECORATION
SLICES OF WATERMELON

Cut the rind off the watermelon. Chop the watermelon into chunks,
discarding any seeds.

Put the watermelon chunks into a food processor or blender and process until
smooth.

Place ice cubes in the glasses. Pour the watermelon mixture over the ice and
serve decorated with slices of melon.

Melon & Mango Tango

BOTH WATERMELONS AND CANTALOUPES ARE AMONG THE MOST THIRST-

QUENCHING FRUITS IN THE WORLD AND ARE PERFECT FOR SUMMER DRINKS.

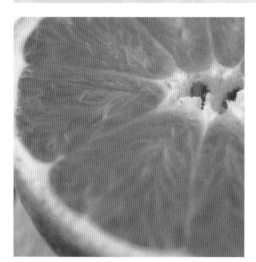

SERVES 2

1 CANTALOUPE MELON, HALVED
  AND SEEDED
2^1/$_2$ CUPS MANGO JUICE
2 TBSP FRESH ORANGE JUICE

DECORATION
SLICES OF ORANGE

Scoop out the melon flesh with a spoon straight into a food processor or blender. Add the mango and orange juices, and process until smooth.

Pour into chilled glasses, decorate with slices of orange, and serve.

Perky Pineapple

THIS IS A GREAT ENERGY BOOSTER AND IS PACKED FULL OF NUTRIENTS. THE TANGY

TASTE IS EXTREMELY REFRESHING AS WELL.

SERVES 4

HANDFUL OF CRACKED ICE

2 BANANAS

1 CUP PINEAPPLE JUICE, CHILLED

1/2 CUP LIME JUICE

DECORATION

SLICES OF PINEAPPLE

Put the cracked ice into a food processor or blender. Peel the bananas and slice directly into the food procesor or blender. Add the pineapple and lime juice, and process until smooth.

Pour into chilled glasses, decorate with slices of pineapple, and serve.

Cool Cranberries

SOFT FRUITS MAKE WONDERFULLY COLORFUL AND TASTY DRINKS. THIS IS
A GREAT WAY TO ENCOURAGE YOUR CHILDREN TO EAT MORE FRUIT.

SERVES **4**

3 CUPS CRANBERRIES, THAWED
  IF FROZEN
SCANT **2** CUPS CRANBERRY JUICE,
  CHILLED
1¼ CUPS PLAIN YOGURT
2–3 TBSP HONEY

Place the berries and juice into a food processor or blender and process again
until combined. Taste and add more honey, if necessary.

Pour into chilled glasses and serve.

Strawberry Colada

STRAWBERRIES ARE A DELICIOUS SOURCE OF IRON, POTASSIUM, AND VITAMINS A AND C.

SERVES **2**

4 CUPS STRAWBERRIES

1/2 CUP COCONUT CREAM

2 1/2 CUPS PINEAPPLE
  JUICE, CHILLED

Reserve 4 strawberries to decorate. Halve the remainder and place in a food processor or blender.

Add the coconut cream and pineapple juice and process until smooth, then pour into chilled glasses, decorate with the reserved strawberries, and serve.

Watermelon Sunset

THE SEEDS OF A WATERMELON CAN BE ROASTED AND EATEN, AND IN FACT THE RIND CAN BE USED TO MAKE PICKLES AND RELISHES, MAKING EVERY PART OF THE FRUIT EDIBLE.

SERVES 4

1 WATERMELON, HALVED
6 TBSP FRESH RUBY GRAPEFRUIT JUICE
6 TBSP FRESH ORANGE JUICE
DASH OF LIME JUICE

DECORATION
SLICES OF WATERMELON

Deseed the melon if you are unable to find a seedless one. Scoop the flesh into a food processor or blender and add the grapefruit juice, orange juice and a dash of lime juice.

Process until smooth, pour into chilled glasses, decorate with slices of watermelon and serve.

Apple Cooler

THE DISTINCTIVE FLAVOR OF FRAGRANT, RIPE APPLES COMBINES WITH FRESH STRAWBERRIES AND FRESHLY SQUEEZED ORANGE JUICE TO GIVE YOU A REALLY ZINGY SMOOTHIE.

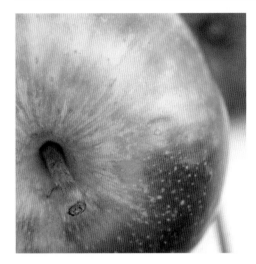 

SERVES **2**

2 RIPE APPLES, PEELED
  AND ROUGHLY CHOPPED
1/4 CUP STRAWBERRIES, HULLED
JUICE OF 4 ORANGES
SUGAR, TO TASTE

DECORATION
SLICES OF APPLE

Put the apples, strawberries, and orange juice into a food processor or blender and process until smooth.

Taste and sweeten with sugar if necessary.

Decorate with slices of apple and serve at once.

Lemon Surprise

ALTHOUGH RICH IN VITAMIN C AND LOW IN CALORIES, LEMON JUICE IS TOO SOUR TO DRINK ON ITS OWN. HERE IT IS PARTNERED WITH PARSLEY, WHICH ALSO HAS HEALTH-GIVING PROPERTIES.

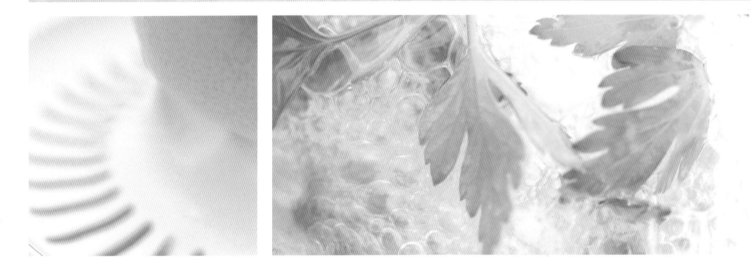

SERVES 2

JUICE OF 1 LEMON
1 TBSP CHOPPED FRESH PARSLEY
SCANT 2 CUPS SPARKLING MINERAL
    WATER
2–3 TSP SUGAR

Put the lemon juice, parsley, and mineral water into a food processor or blender and process on low speed until combined.

Switch the blender to high speed, add the sugar through the feeder tube, and process for 30 seconds more.

Pour into chilled glasses, add straws, and serve.

Melon & Mint Cooler

THE AROMATIC, SWEET-FLESHED, JUICY CANTALOUPE MELON IS THE PERFECT

CHOICE FOR A REFRESHING AND HEALTHY SUMMER DRINK.

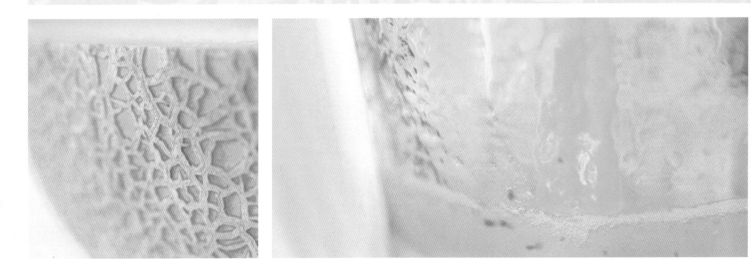

SERVES 2

1 CANTALOUPE MELON
1 TBSP CHOPPED FRESH MINT
1 TBSP CHOPPED PRESERVED GINGER
$1/2$–$2/3$ CUP MINERAL WATER

Halve the melon and scoop out and discard the seeds. Scoop out the flesh and chop coarsely.

Put the melon, mint, and ginger into a food processor or blender and process until smooth and thoroughly combined. With the motor running, add the mineral water, a little at a time, until the mixture reaches the consistency that suits you.

Pour into chilled glasses, add straws, and serve.

Maidenly Mimosa

THIS NON-ALCOHOLIC "COCKTAIL" IS A DELICIOUS ALTERNATIVE FOR NON-DRINKERS AND DRIVERS AT A BRUNCH OR LUNCH PARTY.

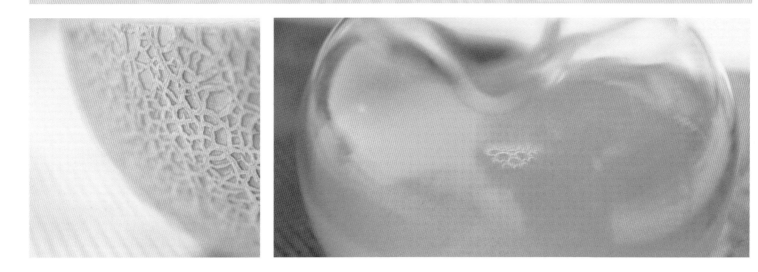

SERVES 2

3/4 CUP FRESHLY SQUEEZED
ORANGE JUICE

3/4 CUP SPARKLING WHITE
GRAPE JUICE

Divide the orange juice between 2 chilled wine glasses or champagne flutes.

Top up with the grape juice and serve.

Peach & Red Currant Sunset

MAKE SURE THE PEACHES YOU USE ARE PROPERLY RIPE SO THEIR FLAVOR COUNTERACTS THE ACIDITY OF THE RED CURRANTS. THIS CLASSIC COMBINATION OF FLAVORS MAKES A VERY PRETTY SMOOTHIE.

SERVES 2

2 LARGE RIPE PEACHES
GENEROUS 2/3 CUP RED CURRANTS
3/4 CUP ICE-COLD WATER
1–2 TBSP HONEY

Halve the peaches and discard the pits. Coarsely chop the peaches and put into the food processor.

Keep 2 stems of red currants whole for decoration and strip the rest off their stems into a food processor or blender. Add the water and honey, and process until smooth.

Pour into glasses and decorate with the remaining red currant sprigs.

Pineapple Crush

THE COMBINATION OF ORANGE JUICE, PINEAPPLE, AND MELON MAKES THIS A REALLY REFRESHING DRINK ON A HOT SUMMER'S DAY.

SERVES 2

SCANT ½ CUP PINEAPPLE JUICE

4 TBSP ORANGE JUICE

4½ OZ/125 G GALIA MELON,
   CUT INTO CHUNKS

5 OZ/140 G FROZEN
   PINEAPPLE CHUNKS

4 ICE CUBES

DECORATION

SLICES OF ORANGE

Pour the pineapple juice and orange juice into a food processor or blender and process gently until combined.

Add the melon, pineapple chunks, and ice cubes, and process until a slushy consistency has been reached.

Pour the mixture into glasses and decorate with slices of orange. Serve at once.

Pomegranate Passion

THIS IS A LOVELY LATE SUMMER DRINK MADE WITH THE NEW SEASON'S POMEGRANATES, WHICH START TO APPEAR IN STORES IN AUGUST.

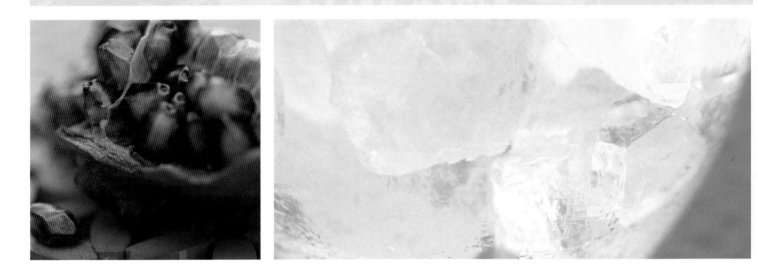

SERVES 2

2 RIPE POMEGRANATES
1 PASSION FRUIT
1 TBSP HONEY
2 GLASSES FULL OF CRUSHED ICE

Cut the pomegranates in half and extract the juice with a basic lemon squeezer.

Halve the passion fruit and strain the pulp into a small bowl. Mix in the pomegranate juice and honey.

Pour over the crushed ice, add straws, and serve.

Raspberry & Apple Quencher

QUICK AND EASY TO MAKE, THIS IS A SIMPLE AND ELEGANT DRINK TO ENJOY.

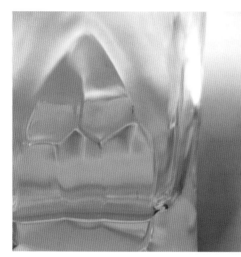 

SERVES 2

8 ICE CUBES, CRUSHED

2 TBSP RASPBERRY SYRUP

GENEROUS 2 CUPS CHILLED
  APPLE JUICE

DECORATION

WHOLE RASPBERRIES AND PIECES
  OF APPLE ON COCKTAIL STICKS

Divide the crushed ice between two glasses and pour over the raspberry syrup.

Top up each glass with chilled apple juice and stir well.

Decorate with the whole raspberries and pieces of apple on cocktail sticks
and serve.

Strawberry Surprise

THIS SUPREMELY THIRST-QUENCHING SMOOTHIE IS IDEAL TO SERVE ON SCORCHING SUMMER
DAYS. THE BALSAMIC VINEGAR BRINGS OUT THE FLAVOR OF THE STRAWBERRIES BEAUTIFULLY.

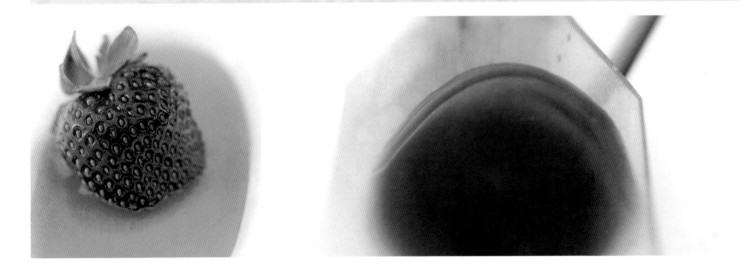

SERVES 2

SCANT 1 CUP FROZEN STRAWBERRIES
GENEROUS 3/4 CUP ICE-COLD WATER
1 TBSP BALSAMIC VINEGAR
1 TBSP FLOWERY HONEY,
    SUCH AS ACACIA

DECORATION
WHOLE STRAWBERRIES

Put the strawberries, water, balsamic vinegar, and honey into a food processor
or blender and process until smooth.

Pour into glasses, decorate with whole strawberries, and serve.

Papaya Sweet & Sour

PAPAYA UNDERGOES AN AMAZING TRANSFORMATION AS IT RIPENS. WITH THE OUTSIDE SKIN YELLOW, THE SOFT RIPE PAPAYA IS A DEEP SUNSET PINK INSIDE.

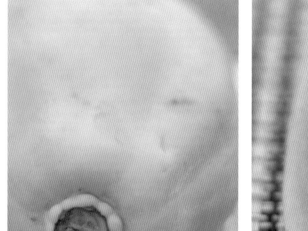 

SERVES 2

9 OZ/250 G RIPE SOFT PAPAYA
3/4 CUP ICE-COLD WATER
JUICE OF 1 LIME

DECORATION
SLICES OF GREEN PAPAYA

Peel the ripe papaya, discarding any seeds. Cut into chunks.

Put the papaya chunks into a food processor or blender with the water and lime, and process until smooth.

Pour into glasses and decorate with slices of green papaya.

Black Grape Fizz

USE LARGE DARK GRAPES FOR THIS FOAMY, REFRESHING COOLER.

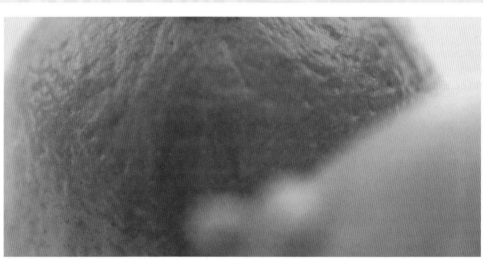

SERVES 2

SCANT 1 CUP BLACK GRAPES,
  DESEEDED OR SEEDLESS
GENEROUS 3/4 CUP SPARKLING
  MINERAL WATER
2 LARGE SCOOPS OF LEMON SHERBET

DECORATION
SLICES OF LIME

Put the grapes, mineral water, and lemon sherbet into a food processor or blender and process until smooth.

Pour into glasses and decorate with slices of lime. Serve immediately.

Raspberry & Black Currant Slush

Fresh, clean, and simple, this is an excellent drink to serve on a really hot day.

SERVES 2

1/2 cup frozen raspberries
1¹/4 cups sparkling mineral water
2 scoops of black currant sherbet

Put the raspberries and water into a food processor or blender and process until smooth.

Add half the sherbet and process briefly until combined with the raspberry mixture.

Pour into glasses, add a scoop of the remaining sherbet to each, and drink while still slushy.

Blood Orange Sparkler

NOW THAT BLOOD (RUBY) ORANGE JUICE IS AVAILABLE ALL YEAR ROUND, YOU

CAN USE ITS FABULOUS COLOR AND FLAVOR WHENEVER YOU WANT.

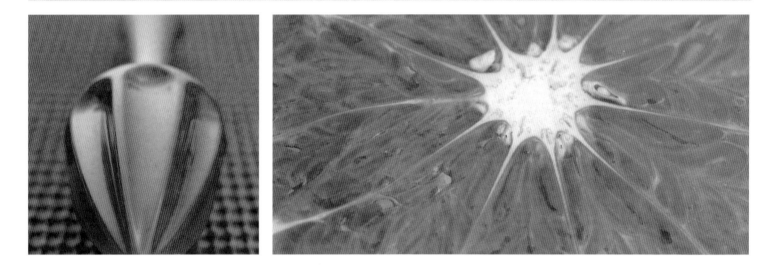

SERVES **2**

1 CUP BLOOD (RUBY) ORANGE JUICE

1 CUP STRAWBERRIES

³/4 CUP RASPBERRIES

¹/4 CUP SPARKLING MINERAL WATER

Put the blood orange juice, strawberries, raspberries, and mineral water into a food processor or blender and process until smooth. Strain the mixture to remove the seeds, if preferred.

Pour into glasses, add straws, and serve.

Strawberry & Pineapple Refresher

LONG-LIFE PINEAPPLE JUICE AND FROZEN FRUIT ARE USED IN THIS EASY-TO-ASSEMBLE

PANTRY SMOOTHIE—THE FLAVORS ARE NOT COMPROMISED BY YOUR HASTE!

SERVES 2

1 CUP FROZEN STRAWBERRIES
1 1/4 CUPS LONG-LIFE PINEAPPLE JUICE
1 TBSP SUPERFINE SUGAR

DECORATION
WEDGES OF PINEAPPLE

Put the strawberries, pineapple juice, and superfine sugar into a food processor or blender and blend until smooth.

Pour into glasses, decorate with wedges of pineapple, and serve.

Perfect Pick-Me-Ups!

Midsummer Smoothie

SMOOTHIES PROVIDE A QUICK, HEALTHY, AND DELICIOUS DRINK THAT'S BOTH FILLING AND NUTRITIOUS — IDEAL WHEN THERE IS NO TIME TO SIT AND EAT, OR AS A REFRESHING EARLY MORNING APPETIZER.

SERVES 2

GENEROUS 3/4 CUP STRAWBERRIES

GENEROUS 3/4 CUP RASPBERRIES

3/8 CUP BLUEBERRIES

1 RIPE PASSION FRUIT

2/3 CUP MILK

DECORATION

VANILLA AND STRAWBERRY
   ICE CREAM

Lightly rinse the strawberries, raspberries, and blueberries, and scoop out the passion fruit pulp. Place all the fruits in a food processor or blender and blend for 1 minute. Add the milk and blend again.

Pour into glasses and serve with a scoop of vanilla and strawberry ice cream on top of each.

Mango & Orange Smoothie

IF YOU WANT A CREAMY SMOOTHIE, USE VANILLA ICE CREAM INSTEAD OF MANGO SHERBET. THE MANGO MUST BE QUITE RIPE AND FRAGRANT. IT SHOULD BE SOFT AND YIELD TO GENTLE PRESSURE.

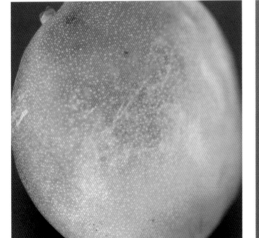 

SERVES 2

1 LARGE RIPE MANGO
JUICE OF 2 MEDIUM ORANGES
3 SCOOPS OF MANGO SHERBET

DECORATION
STRIPS OF ORANGE ZEST

Place the mango on a cutting board and cut lengthwise through the flesh as close to the large flat central pit as possible. Turn it over and do the same thing on the other side of the pit. Remove the peel and coarsely chop the flesh before placing in a food processor or blender.

Add the orange juice and sherbet and process until smooth.

Serve at once, decorated with strips of orange zest.

Pear, Orange & Ginger Reviver

PRETTY AND FRAGRANT, WITH THE WARMTH OF GINGER, THIS SMOOTHIE WILL

BRIGHTEN A LESS THAN PERFECT SUMMER'S DAY.

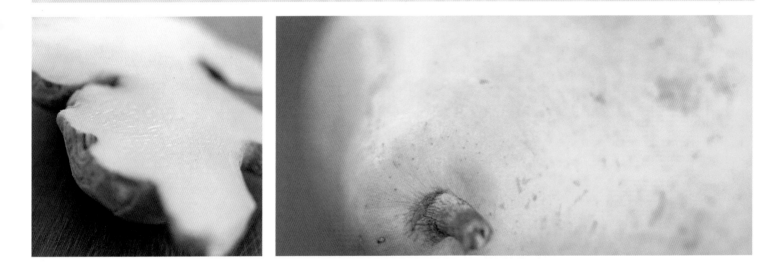

SERVES 2

2 LARGE RIPE BARTLETT
  OR SIMILAR JUICY PEARS
JUICE OF 4 MEDIUM ORANGES
4 CUBES CANDIED GINGER

Peel the pears and cut into fourths, removing the cores. Put into a food processor or blender with the orange juice and the candied ginger, and process until smooth.

Pour into glasses and serve.

Honeydew

THE NATURAL TEXTURE OF THE HONEYDEW MELON LENDS ITSELF TO THIS DELICATE SMOOTHIE. FOR BEST RESULTS, MAKE SURE THE MELON IS TRULY RIPE.

SERVES 2

9 OZ/250 G HONEYDEW MELON
1¹/₄ CUPS SPARKLING MINERAL WATER
2 TBSP HONEY

DECORATION
RED CURRANT CLUSTERS

Cut the rind off the melon. Chop the melon into chunks, discarding any seeds.

Put into a food processor or blender with the water and honey, and process until smooth.

Pour into glasses and decorate with clusters of red currants.

Summer Fruit Slush

THIS MEDLEY OF SUMMER BERRIES MAKES AN INSPIRED DRINK.

SERVES **2**

4 TBSP ORANGE JUICE

1 TBSP LIME JUICE

SCANT $^1/_2$ CUP SPARKLING WATER

2$^1/_3$ CUPS FROZEN SUMMER FRUITS
  (SUCH AS BLUEBERRIES,
  RASPBERRIES, BLACKBERRIES,
  AND STRAWBERRIES)

4 ICE CUBES

Pour the orange juice, lime juice, and sparkling water into a food processor or blender and process gently until combined.

Add the summer fruits and ice cubes, and process until a slushy consistency has been reached.

Pour the mixture into glasses and serve.

Forest Fruit Smoothie

THIS DRINK COMBINES THE RICH FLAVORS AND COLORS OF FOREST FRUITS IN ONE
SUPERB SMOOTHIE.

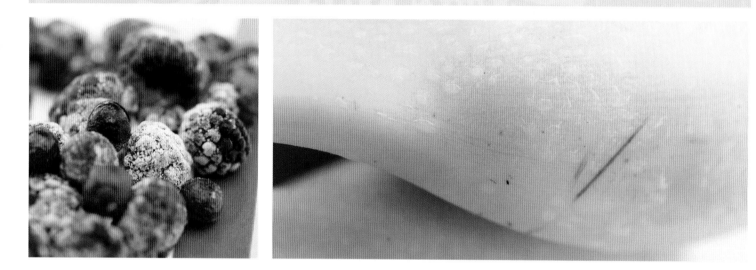

SERVES 2

1¹/₂ CUPS ORANGE JUICE

1 BANANA, SLICED AND FROZEN

3 CUPS FROZEN FOREST FRUITS
   (SUCH AS BLUEBERRIES, RASPBERRIES,
   AND BLACKBERRIES)

DECORATION

SLICES OF FRESH ORANGE

Pour the orange juice into a food processor or blender. Add the banana and
half of the forest fruits, and process until smooth.

Add the remaining forest fruits and process until smooth. Pour the mixture
into tall glasses and decorate the rims with slices of fresh orange.

Add straws and serve.

Melon Refresher

INCORPORATING THREE DIFFERENT TYPES OF MELONS, THE FLAVOR OF THIS

SMOOTHIE IS BOTH DELICATE AND REFRESHING ON A HOT DAY.

SERVES 2

1 CUP PLAIN YOGURT

3¹/2 OZ/100 G GALIA MELON,
   CUT INTO CHUNKS

3¹/2 OZ/100 G CANTALOUPE MELON,
   CUT INTO CHUNKS

3¹/2 OZ/100 G WATERMELON,
   CUT INTO CHUNKS

6 ICE CUBES, CRUSHED

DECORATION

WEDGES OF MELON

Pour the yogurt into a food processor or blender. Add the galia melon chunks and process until smooth.

Add the cantaloupe and watermelon chunks along with the ice cubes, and process until smooth.

Pour the mixture into glasses and decorate with wedges of melon.

Serve at once.

Homemade Lemonade

THIS CLASSIC COOLER IS A WELL-LOVED, TRADITIONAL FAVORITE.

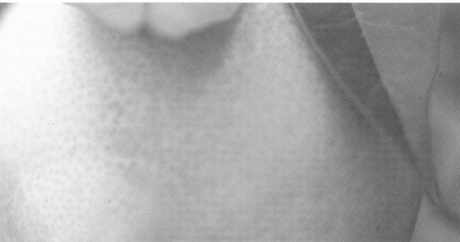

SERVES 2

2/3 CUP WATER

6 TBSP SUGAR

1 TSP GRATED LEMON RIND

1/2 CUP LEMON JUICE

6 ICE CUBES

TO SERVE

SPARKLING WATER

DECORATION

GRANULATED SUGAR

SLICES OF LEMON

Put the water, sugar, and grated lemon rind into a small pan and bring to a boil, stirring constantly. Continue to boil, stirring, for 5 minutes.

Remove from the heat and let cool to room temperature. Stir in the lemon juice, then transfer to a pitcher and cover with plastic wrap. Chill in the refrigerator for at least 2 hours.

When the lemonade has almost finished chilling, take two glasses and rub the rims with a wedge of lemon, then dip them in granulated sugar to frost. Put the ice cubes into the glasses.

Remove the lemon syrup from the refrigerator, then pour it over the ice and top up with sparkling water. The ratio should be one part lemon syrup to three parts sparkling water. Stir well to mix. Decorate with sugar and slices of fresh lemon and serve.

Cranberry Energizer

SWEET AND SOUR COMBINE TO MAKE A DELICIOUSLY ENERGIZING JUICE PACKED

FULL OF GOODNESS.

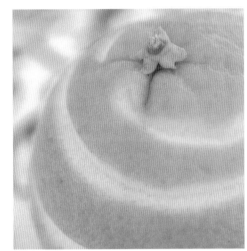 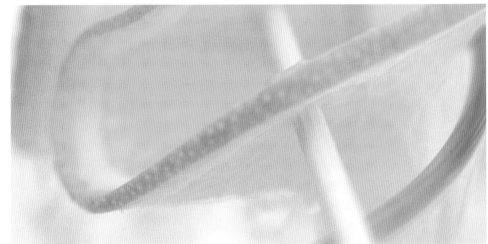

SERVES 2

1^{1}/$_{4}$ CUPS CRANBERRY JUICE
SCANT ^{1}/$_{2}$ CUP ORANGE JUICE
1 CUP FRESH RASPBERRIES
1 TBSP LEMON JUICE

DECORATION
SLICES AND SPIRALS OF FRESH
  LEMON OR ORANGE

Pour the cranberry juice and orange juice into a food processor or blender and process gently until combined. Add the raspberries and lemon juice, and process until smooth.

Pour the mixture into glasses and decorate with slices and spirals of fresh lemon or orange. Serve at once.

Cherry Sour

USE THE BOTTLING LIQUID AS WELL AS THE FRUIT FOR THIS SHARP,

THIRST-QUENCHING SMOOTHIE.

SERVES 2

9 OZ/250 G BOTTLED MORELLO
  CHERRIES
2/3 CUP STRAINED PLAIN YOGURT
SUGAR, TO TASTE

DECORATION
CHERRIES ON COCKTAIL STICKS

Put the cherries with their bottling liquid into a food processor or blender with the yogurt, then process until smooth.

Taste and sweeten with sugar if necessary.

Pour into glasses and serve. Decorate with cherries on cocktail sticks.

Banana & Apple Booster

GINGER AND CINNAMON SPICE UP THESE EVERYDAY FRUITS TO MAKE A GREAT

ENERGIZER FOR A COLD WINTER MORNING.

 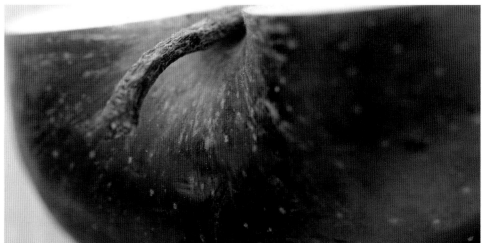

SERVES 2

1 CUP APPLE JUICE

$^1/_2$ TSP POWDERED CINNAMON

2 TSP GRATED FRESH GINGERROOT

2 BANANAS, SLICED AND FROZEN

DECORATION

CHUNKS OF FRESH APPLE ON
 COCKTAIL STICKS

Pour the apple juice into a food processor or blender. Add the cinnamon and ginger, and process gently until combined.

Add the bananas and process until smooth. Pour the mixture into tall glasses and decorate with chunks of fresh apple on cocktail sticks. Serve at once.

Black Currant Bracer

PURPLE PASSION! FOR A STRICTLY GROWN-UP VERSION, USE CRÈME DE CASSIS INSTEAD OF THE CORDIAL.

SERVES **2**

2/3 CUP FROZEN BLACK CURRANTS

4 SCOOPS OF BLACK CURRANT
   SHERBET

SCANT 1/2 CUP SOUR CREAM

2 TBSP BLACK CURRANT CORDIAL,
   PLUS EXTRA FOR DRIZZLING

1 TBSP WATER

SUGAR, TO TASTE

DECORATION

A FEW MINT LEAVES

WHOLE BLACKBERRIES

Put the black currants, sherbet, sour cream, cordial, and water into a food processor or blender and process until smooth. Taste and sweeten with a little sugar if necessary.

Pour into glasses. Drizzle over some cordial, decorate with the mint leaves and blackberries, and serve.

Kiwi Cooler

USE A STRAWBERRY ICE CREAM TO CONTRAST WITH THE GLORIOUS GREEN COLOR OF THIS SMOOTHIE, OR A LIME SHERBET TO TONE IN WITH IT. WHICHEVER YOU CHOOSE, THE COMBINATION WILL BE DELIGHTFUL.

SERVES 2

4 RIPE KIWI FRUIT, PEELED AND CUT INTO FOURTHS

GENEROUS 3/4 CUP TRADITIONAL SPARKLING LEMONADE

DECORATION
2 LARGE SCOOPS OF ICE CREAM OR SHERBET

Put the kiwi fruit and lemonade into a food processor or blender and process until smooth.

Pour into glasses and top with a scoop of ice cream or sherbet.

Serve at once.

Pineapple Tango

THIS LONG, COOL, THIRST-QUENCHER WILL REVITALIZE YOU WHEN YOU ARE

FEELING TIRED OR STRESSED.

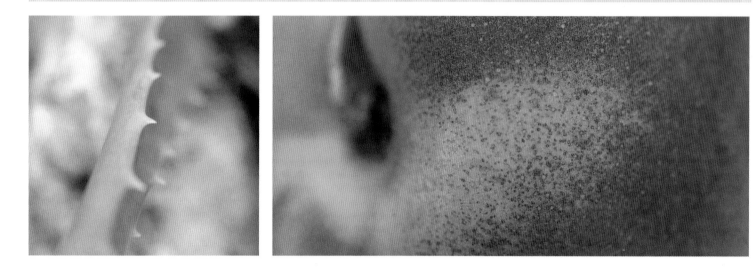

SERVES **2**

$^1/_2$ CUP PINEAPPLE JUICE

JUICE OF **1** LEMON

SCANT $^1/_2$ CUP WATER

3 TBSP BROWN SUGAR

GENEROUS $^3/_4$ CUP PLAIN YOGURT

1 PEACH, CUT INTO CHUNKS AND
  FROZEN

$^3/_4$ CUP FROZEN PINEAPPLE CHUNKS

DECORATION

WEDGES OF FRESH PINEAPPLE

Pour the pineapple juice, lemon juice, and water into a food processor or blender. Add the sugar and yogurt, and process until blended.

Add the peach and pineapple chunks, and process until smooth.

Pour the mixture into glasses and decorate the rims with wedges of fresh pineapple.

Serve at once.

White Grape Elderflower Foam

Use Champagne or Muscat grapes to add to the delicate floweriness of this light smoothie.

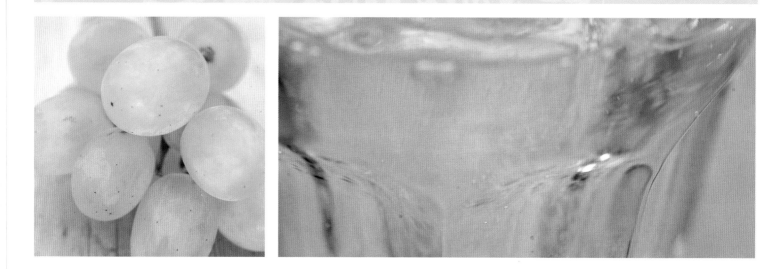

SERVES 2

GENEROUS 1/2 CUP WHITE GRAPES,
  DESEEDED OR SEEDLESS
GENEROUS 3/4 CUP SPARKLING
  MINERAL WATER
2 LARGE SCOOPS OF
  FROZEN YOGURT (PLAIN)
1 1/2 TBSP ELDERFLOWER CORDIAL

DECORATION
WHITE GRAPES

Put the grapes, mineral water, frozen yogurt, and elderflower cordial into a food processor or blender and process until smooth.

Pour into glasses, add a few grapes, and serve immediately.

Elderflower & Pear Smoothie

MAKE THIS SMOOTHIE IN LATE SPRING OR EARLY SUMMER WHEN THE ELDER BUSHES ARE IN FULL BLOOM.

SERVES 2

4 SMALL FIRM PEARS

2 HEADS OF ELDER FLOWERS, FRESHLY PICKED (OR A DASH OF CORDIAL)

1 STRIP OF LEMON ZEST

1 TBSP SOFT BROWN SUGAR

4 TBSP WATER

GENEROUS 3/4 CUP MILK

TO SERVE

CATS' TONGUES

Peel the pears and cut into fourths, discarding the cores. Place in a pan with the elder flowers or cordial, a strip of lemon zest, the sugar, and water. Cover tightly and simmer until the pears are very soft. Let cool.

Discard the elder flowers and lemon zest. Put the pears, cooking liquid, and milk into a food processor or blender and process until smooth.

Serve immediately with cats' tongues.

Fig & Maple Melter

Go on, indulge yourself with this rich, delicious, and sophisticated smoothie.

SERVES 2

1¹/₂ cups hazelnut yogurt

2 tbsp freshly squeezed
  orange juice

4 tbsp maple syrup

8 large fresh figs, chopped

6 ice cubes, crushed

DECORATION

TOASTED CHOPPED HAZELNUTS

Pour the yogurt, orange juice, and maple syrup into a food processor or blender and process gently until combined.

Add the figs and ice cubes, and process until smooth.

Pour the mixture into glasses and scatter over some toasted chopped hazelnuts.

Serve at once.

Green Tea & Yellow Plum Smoothie

THE HAUNTING FLAVOR OF GREEN TEA COMBINES BRILLIANTLY WITH GOLDEN-YELLOW PLUMS. IF THE WEATHER ISN'T WONDERFUL, THIS SMOOTHIE IS JUST AS DELICIOUS SERVED WARM.

SERVES 2

1 GREEN TEA WITH EASTERN
  SPICE TEA BAG
1¼ CUPS BOILING WATER
1 TBSP SUGAR
²/₃ CUP RIPE YELLOW PLUMS,
  HALVED AND PITTED

Put the tea bag in a teapot or heatproof pitcher and pour over the boiling water. Let infuse for 7 minutes. Remove and discard the tea bag. Let chill.

Pour the chilled tea into a food processor or blender. Add the sugar and plums, and process until smooth.

Serve at once.

Super Shakes!

Chocolate Milkshake

THE ULTIMATE MILKSHAKE FOR CHILDREN AND CHOCOHOLICS ALIKE, THIS DRINK IS SUPREMELY SATISFYING.

SERVES 2

2/3 CUP MILK

2 TBSP CHOCOLATE SYRUP

14 OZ/400 G CHOCOLATE ICE
    CREAM

DECORATION

GRATED CHOCOLATE

Pour the milk and chocolate syrup into a food processor or blender and process gently until combined.

Add the chocolate ice cream and process until smooth. Pour the mixture into tall glasses and scatter the grated chocolate over the shakes.

Serve at once.

Spiced Banana Milkshake

THIS IS A CARIBBEAN COMBINATION OF FRUIT AND SPICES THAT WILL TANTALIZE

THE TASTEBUDS.

SERVES 2

1¹/₄ CUPS MILK
¹/₂ TSP ALLSPICE
5¹/₂ OZ/150 G BANANA ICE CREAM
2 BANANAS, SLICED AND FROZEN

Pour the milk into a food processor or blender. Add the allspice. Add half of the banana ice cream and process gently until combined, then add the remaining ice cream and process until well blended.

When the mixture is well combined, add the bananas and process until smooth.

DECORATION
PINCH OF ALLSPICE

Pour the mixture into glasses, add a pinch of allspice to decorate, and serve.

Strawberries & Cream Milkshake

The ultimate strawberry milkshake! Forget about synthetic strawberry-flavored syrups—this is the real thing: a gorgeous flavor and fantastically fruity. Set off the pale coloring with some pretty green mint leaves.

SERVES 2

1 CUP FROZEN STRAWBERRIES

SCANT $^{1}/_{2}$ CUP LIGHT CREAM

GENEROUS $^{3}/_{4}$ CUP COLD WHOLE MILK

1 TBSP SUPERFINE SUGAR

DECORATION

MINT LEAVES

Put the strawberries, cream, milk, and superfine sugar into a food processor or blender and process until smooth.

Pour into glasses and serve decorated with mint leaves.

Smooth Nectarine Shake

MANGO AND NECTARINE IS AN INSPIRED COMBINATION OF FRUITS, MADE ALL THE
MORE SPECIAL WITH THE CLEVER ADDITION OF LEMON SHERBET.

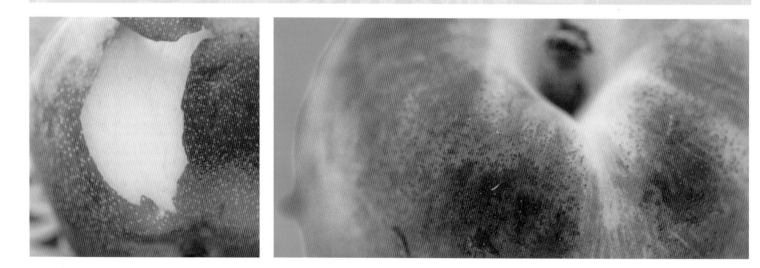

SERVES 2

1 CUP MILK
12 OZ/350 G LEMON SHERBET
1 RIPE MANGO, PITTED AND DICED
2 RIPE NECTARINES, PITTED AND DICED

DECORATION
THIN WEDGES OF NECTARINE

Pour the milk into a food processor or blender, then add half of the lemon
sherbet and process gently until combined. Add the remaining sherbet and
process until smooth.

When the mixture is thoroughly blended, gradually add the mango and
nectarines and process until smooth.

Pour the mixture into glasses, decorate with thin wedges of nectarine,
and serve.

Tropical Storm

REVIVE YOURSELF WITH THIS INVIGORATING AND EXUBERANT TROPICAL SHAKE.

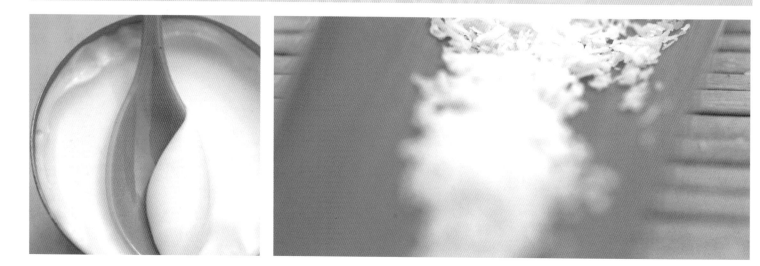

SERVES 2

1 CUP MILK

SCANT $^{1}/_{2}$ CUP COCONUT MILK

5$^{1}/_{2}$ OZ/150 G VANILLA ICE CREAM

2 BANANAS, SLICED AND FROZEN

SCANT 1$^{1}/_{2}$ CUPS CANNED PINEAPPLE
   CHUNKS, DRAINED

1 PAPAYA, DESEEDED AND DICED

DECORATION

GRATED FRESH COCONUT

Pour the milk and coconut milk into a food processor or blender and process gently until combined. Add half of the ice cream and process gently, then add the remaining ice cream and process until smooth.

Add the bananas and process well, then add the pineapple chunks and papaya and process until smooth.

Pour the mixture into tall glasses, scatter the grated coconut over the shakes, and serve.

Peach Bliss

DIFFERENT FRUITS COMBINE WITH PEACHES TO MAKE ONE MARVELOUSLY

FRUITY DRINK.

SERVES 2

3/4 CUP MILK

1 CUP CANNED PEACH
  SLICES, DRAINED

2 FRESH APRICOTS, CHOPPED

2²/3 CUPS FRESH STRAWBERRIES,
  HULLED AND SLICED

2 BANANAS, SLICED AND FROZEN

DECORATION

SLICES OF NECTARINE, STRAWBERRIES,
  AND BANANA ON COCKTAIL STICKS

Pour the milk into a food processor or blender. Add the peach slices and process gently until combined. Add the apricots and process gently until combined.

Add the strawberries and banana slices, and process until smooth.

Pour the mixture into glasses and decorate with the fruit speared on a cocktail stick.

Serve at once.

Perfect Plum Shake

A DEEP, RICH, AND FRUITY SHAKE FOR THE END OF THE SUMMER.

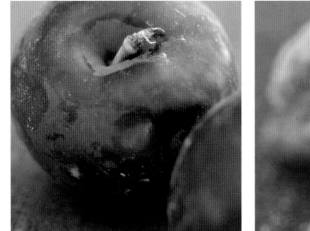

SERVES 2

9 OZ/250 G RIPE PLUMS

GENEROUS 3/4 CUP WATER

1 TBSP GOLDEN GRANULATED SUGAR

4 SCOOPS OF FROZEN YOGURT
(PLAIN) OR ICE CREAM

2 ITALIAN ALMOND OR
PISTACHIO BISCOTTI, CRUMBLED

TO SERVE

EXTRA BISCOTTI, CRUMBLED

DECORATION

PLUMS, WHOLE OR CUT IN HALF

Put the plums, water, and sugar into a small pan. Cover tightly and simmer for about 15 minutes, or until the plums have split and are very soft. Let cool.

Strain off the liquid into a food processor or blender and add the frozen yogurt or ice cream. Process until smooth and frothy.

Pour into glasses and decorate the rims with whole or halved plums. Sprinkle with the crumbled biscotti and serve with extra biscotti on the side.

Raspberry Ripple Rice Cream

A FRESH-TASTING, NONDAIRY SHAKE WITH NO ANIMAL PRODUCTS, NO CHOLESTEROL, NO LACTOSE, AND NO PROBLEM! RICE "MILK" SHOULD BE KEPT COLD IN THE REFRIGERATOR FOR THE BEST-TASTING RESULTS. SOY MILK CAN BE USED INSTEAD, BUT THE RICE "MILK" TASTES MUCH NICER.

SERVES 2

GENEROUS 3/4 CUP FROZEN
  RASPBERRIES
1 1/4 CUPS RICE "MILK" OR SOY MILK

Put the raspberries and half the rice "milk" into a food processor or blender and process until smooth.

Strain into a pitcher and carefully stir through the remaining rice "milk" to give a marbled effect.

Pour into glasses and serve.

Coffee Banana Cooler

A POWERHOUSE FOR THOSE WHO LEAD AN ACTIVE LIFE — THIS MILKSHAKE TASTES FABULOUS, TOO.

SERVES 2

1¹/₄ CUPS MILK

4 TBSP INSTANT COFFEE POWDER

5¹/₂ OZ/150 G VANILLA ICE CREAM

2 BANANAS, SLICED AND FROZEN

Pour the milk into a food processor or blender, then add the coffee powder and process gently until combined. Add half of the vanilla ice cream and process gently, then add the remaining ice cream and process until well combined.

When the mixture is thoroughly blended, add the bananas and process until smooth.

Pour the mixture into glasses and serve.

Plum Fluff

You will need perfectly ripe plums for this fabulously frothy, fruity recipe. Dark ones—such as Marjorie's Seedling—give a better color.

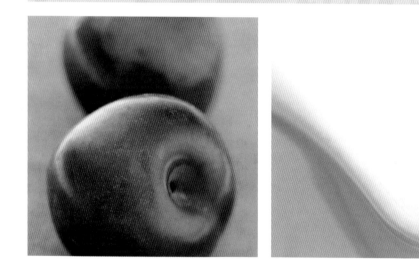

SERVES 2

4 MEDIUM RIPE PLUMS, PITTED
GENEROUS 3/4 CUP ICE-COLD MILK
2 SCOOPS OF LUXURY VANILLA ICE
   CREAM

TO SERVE
CRUMBLY OAT COOKIES

Put the plums, milk, and ice cream into a food processor or blender and process until smooth and frothy.

Pour into glasses and serve at once with crumbly oat cookies.

Peach & Orange Milkshake

A LUSCIOUS COMBINATION OF FRUITS TO LEAVE YOU RESTORED, REVIVED, AND REFRESHED.

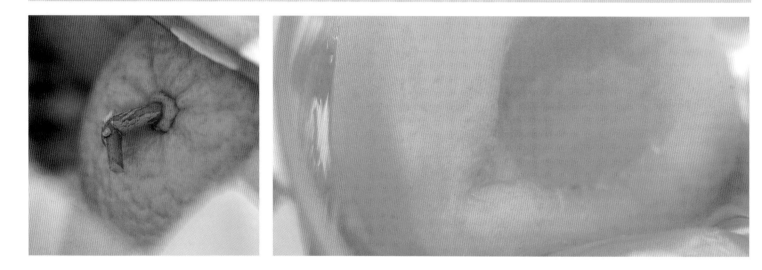

SERVES 2

SCANT $^1/_2$ CUP MILK

$^1/_2$ CUP PEACH YOGURT

SCANT $^1/_2$ CUP ORANGE JUICE

1 CUP CANNED PEACH SLICES, DRAINED

6 ICE CUBES, CRUSHED

DECORATION

STRIPS OF ORANGE PEEL

Pour the milk, yogurt, and orange juice into a food processor or blender and process gently until combined.

Add the peach slices and ice cubes, and process until smooth. Pour the mixture into glasses and decorate with strips of orange peel.

Black & White Smoothie

CHOCOLATE AND CHERRIES ARE A CLASSIC COMBINATION. YOU CAN ALSO SERVE THIS WHITE CHOCOLATE AND BLACK CHERRY SMOOTHIE AS A DESSERT, WITH A COUPLE OF DARK CHOCOLATE THINS.

SERVES 2

3/4 CUP BLACK CHERRIES

3 LARGE SCOOPS OF LUXURY
  WHITE CHOCOLATE ICE CREAM

2/3 CUP MILK

Halve and pit the black cherries. Put these into a food processor or blender and process until puréed.

Add the ice cream and milk, and process briefly to mix well.

Pour into glasses and serve.

Creamy Maple Shake

MAPLE, VANILLA, AND ALMOND ARE DELICATE FLAVORS THAT COMPLEMENT EACH OTHER PERFECTLY.

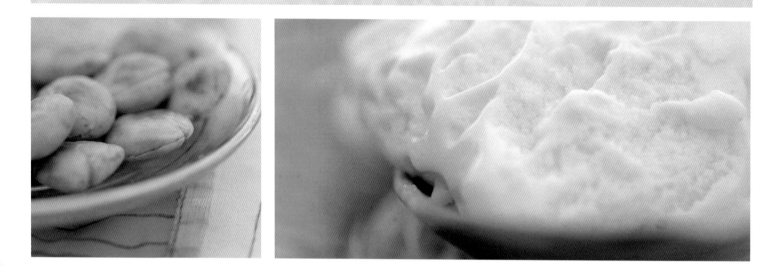

SERVES 2

2/3 CUP MILK

2 TBSP MAPLE SYRUP

14 OZ/400 G VANILLA ICE CREAM

1 TBSP ALMOND EXTRACT

DECORATION

CHOPPED ALMONDS

Pour the milk and maple syrup into a food processor or blender and process gently until combined.

Add the ice cream and almond extract, and process until smooth.

Pour the mixture into glasses, scatter the chopped nuts over the shakes, and serve.

Kiwi & Lime Shake

THIS DRINK PROVIDES A GOOD SOURCE OF VITAMIN C, AS WELL AS A
WONDERFULLY REFRESHING SWEET AND SHARP FLAVOR.

SERVES 2

²/₃ CUP MILK

JUICE OF 2 LIMES

2 KIWI FRUIT, CHOPPED

1 TBSP SUGAR

14 OZ/400 G VANILLA ICE CREAM

DECORATION

SLICES OF KIWI FRUIT

STRIPS OF LIME PEEL

Pour the milk and lime juice into a food processor or blender and process gently until combined.

Add the kiwi fruit and sugar and process gently, then add the ice cream and process until smooth.

Pour the mixture into glasses and decorate with slices of kiwi fruit and strips of lime peel.

Serve at once.

Peppermint Refresher

SURPRISINGLY BOTH HOT AND COLD ON THE TONGUE, THIS MINTY COOLER WILL

RESTORE VITALITY AND VIGOR.

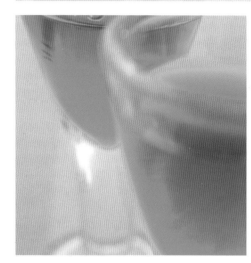 

SERVES **2**

^{2}/3 CUP MILK

2 TBSP PEPPERMINT SYRUP

14 OZ/400 G PEPPERMINT ICE
 CREAM

DECORATION

SPRIGS OF FRESH MINT

Pour the milk and peppermint syrup into a food processor or blender and process gently until combined.

Add the peppermint ice cream and process until smooth.

Pour the mixture into tall glasses and decorate with sprigs of fresh mint.

Coconut Cream

AN INVIGORATING AND CREAMY SMOOTHIE TO LIFT YOUR MOOD AND REMIND YOU OF TROPICAL BEACHES.

SERVES 2

1^1/$_2$ CUPS PINEAPPLE JUICE

^{1}/$_3$ CUP COCONUT MILK

5^1/$_2$ OZ/150 G VANILLA ICE CREAM

1 CUP FROZEN PINEAPPLE CHUNKS

DECORATION

2 TBSP GRATED FRESH COCONUT

TO SERVE

2 SCOOPED-OUT COCONUT SHELLS
  (OPTIONAL)

Pour the pineapple juice and coconut milk into a food processor or blender. Add the ice cream and process until smooth.

Add the pineapple chunks and process until smooth.

Pour the mixture into scooped-out coconut shells, or tall glasses, and decorate with grated fresh coconut.

Add straws and serve.

Fuzzy Peg

A CHILD'S DELIGHT BOTH IN TASTE AND ITS INCREDIBLY STRANGE APPEARANCE! IT COULD BE MADE WITH OTHER DRINKS, TOO.

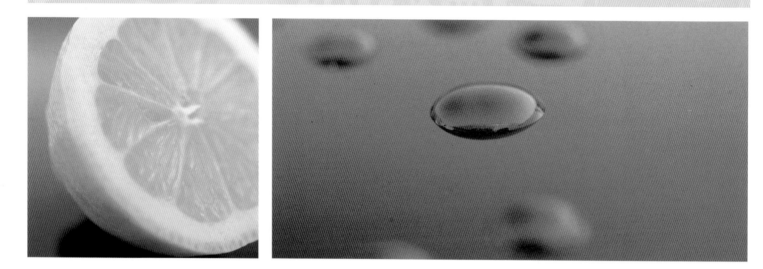

SERVES 1

2 SCOOPS VANILLA ICE CREAM
1 MEASURE LIME OR LEMON
  JUICE CORDIAL
COLA
ICE

Blend the ice cream and lime or lemon juice cordial together for 5–10 seconds with a little cola.

Pour into a tall glass filled with ice and top up with cola.

Drink through straws.

Mocha Cream

THE HEAVENLY PAIRING OF COFFEE AND CHOCOLATE CAN BE IMPROVED ONLY BY
THE ADDITION OF WHIPPED CREAM.

SERVES 2

GENEROUS 3/4 CUP MILK

SCANT 1/4 CUP LIGHT CREAM

1 TBSP BROWN SUGAR

2 TBSP UNSWEETENED COCOA

1 TBSP COFFEE SYRUP OR INSTANT
  COFFEE POWDER

6 ICE CUBES

DECORATION

WHIPPED CREAM

GRATED CHOCOLATE

Put the milk, cream, and sugar into a food processor or blender and process
gently until combined.

Add the unsweetened cocoa and coffee syrup or powder and process well,
then add the ice cubes and process until smooth.

Pour the mixture into glasses. Top with whipped cream, then scatter the
grated chocolate over the drinks and serve.

Iced Coffee & Chocolate Crush

COFFEE AND A HINT OF PEPPERMINT COMBINE IN THIS DELICIOUS CRUSH, WHICH IS TOPPED WITH CHOCOLATE.

SERVES 2

1³/4 CUPS MILK

GENEROUS ³/4 CUP COFFEE SYRUP

SCANT ¹/2 CUP PEPPERMINT SYRUP

1 TBSP CHOPPED FRESH MINT LEAVES

4 ICE CUBES, CRUSHED

DECORATION

GRATED CHOCOLATE

SPRIGS OF FRESH MINT

Pour the milk, coffee syrup, and peppermint syrup into a food processor or blender and process gently until combined.

Add the mint and ice cubes, and process until a slushy consistency has been reached.

Pour the mixture into glasses. Scatter over the grated chocolate, then decorate with sprigs of fresh mint and serve.

index